Albert Luthuli

OHIO SHORT HISTORIES OF AFRICA

This series of Ohio Short Histories of Africa is meant for those who are looking for a brief but lively introduction to a wide range of topics in African history, politics, and biography, written by some of the leading experts in their fields.

Albert Luthuli

Robert Trent Vinson

OHIO UNIVERSITY PRESS

ATHENS

Ohio University Press, Athens, Ohio 45701
ohioswallow.com
© 2018 by Ohio University Press

To obtain permission to quote, reprint, or otherwise reproduce or
distribute material from Ohio University Press publications, please
contact our rights and permissions department at (740) 593-1154
or (740) 593-4536 (fax).

Printed in the United States of America
Ohio University Press books are printed on acid-free paper ⊚ ™

28 27 26 25 24 23 22 21 20 19 18   5 4 3 2 1

Library of Congress Cataloging-in-Publication Data:
Names: Vinson, Robert Trent, author.
Title: Albert Luthuli / Robert Trent Vinson.
Other titles: Ohio short histories of Africa.
Description: Athens, Ohio : Ohio University Press, 2018. | Series: Ohio short
   histories of Africa
Identifiers: LCCN 2018019625| ISBN 9780821423288 (pb : alk. paper) | ISBN
   9780821446423 (pdf)
Subjects: LCSH: Luthuli, A. J. (Albert John), 1898-1967. | African National
   Congress--Biography. | Government, Resistance to--South Africa. | South
   Africa--Politics and government--20th century. | South Africa--Race
   relations.
Classification: LCC E184.H95 V56 2018 | DDC 968.05092--dc23
LC record available at https://lccn.loc.gov/2018019625

Contents

Illustrations

Acknowledgments

Many, many people contributed to his project. I first thank Gillian Berchowitz for her initial invitation to write about Albert Luthuli and for her expert and encouraging editorial guidance. Peter Alegi, Jean Allman, Phil Bonner, Benedict Carton, Robert Edgar, Michael Kirkwood, Dingane Mthethwa, Jon Soske, Raymond Suttner, Tyler Thomson, and Wendy Urban-Mead read all or portions of this work, though I remain solely responsible for any errors. I also thank Joel Cabrita, Benedict Carton, Robert Edgar, Natasha Erlank, Abosede George, Michael Gomez, Elizabeth Gunner, Robert Houle, Paul Landau, Peter Limb, E. S. Reddy, Jabulani Sithole, Karin Shapiro, Jon Soske, and Raymond Suttner for stimulating conversations about Luthuli. I also thank the participants at the 2015 Northeastern Workshop on South African History, the African History seminar at Duke University, the African Diaspora seminar at New York University, the African Christianities Conference at Cambridge University, and the Armed Struggle Conference at the University of the Witwatersrand for commenting on earlier iterations of this work. Generous funding from the College of William and Mary made possible research trips to South Africa and the United Kingdom and throughout the United States. I am very grateful to Diana Lachatenere and Steven Fullwood III at the Schomburg Center for Research in Black Culture and especially to Ms. Thandi Luthuli-Gcabashe for making available to me the Albert Luthuli papers deposited there. I am also indebted to Peter Limb for making available the Mary-Louise Hooper papers while they were still being processed. Of course, nothing is possible without the support and eternal love of the Vinson, McClendon, and Harvey families. This book is dedicated to my grandmother, Josephine Vinson, for loving me unconditionally and to my cousin Jean, who was there when I most needed her and whom I miss every single day.

Who Was Albert Luthuli?

When Albert Luthuli, president of the African National Congress (ANC), South Africa's leading antiapartheid organization, became the first African-born recipient of the Nobel Peace Prize in December 1961, the world celebrated his advocacy of nonviolent civil disobedience. The prize signaled international recognition for his Gandhian strategy to end apartheid, South Africa's disastrous white supremacist political policy of racial subordination and separation, and connected South Africa's antiapartheid struggle to the growing global human rights campaigns exemplified by the 1948 United Nations Declaration of Human Rights. It propelled Luthuli to global celebrity and raised the profile of the ANC, which he had led since 1952. The ANC would survive lethal state repression in the 1960s and throughout two ensuing decades. As a mass organization, it articulated a broad, inclusive African nationalism and led the Congress Alliance, a multiracial, multi-ideological antiapartheid coalition that shared Luthuli's vision of a nonracial, democratic, equitable South Africa.

Luthuli's admirers regarded him as a global icon of peace and reconciliation, similar to Mahatma Gandhi and Martin Luther King Jr. More than thirty years before Nelson Mandela walked out of prison in 1990 onto the world stage with his stirring statesman's vision of racial reconciliation in a democratic South Africa, Luthuli was "Mandela before Mandela," adored by Africans, Indians, Coloureds, and an increasing number of whites as a unique unifying figure. At that time, many regarded the ANC president as South Africa's likely political leader if the disenfranchised majority could vote in a post-apartheid, democratic state. Although some regarded Luthuli as a South African version of King, his fellow Nobel laureate declared himself a follower and admirer of Luthuli. Both men shared a vision of universal love and Christian activism against the moral evil of white supremacy, linking South African and American free-dom struggles to decolonization and labor movements in Africa, Asia, and the Caribbean. But while Gandhi facilitated Indian independence, King won major civil rights victories that ended a century of legalized Jim Crow segregation, and Mandela would become South Africa's first democratically elected president, Luthuli's extraordinary statesmanship did not result in similar victories. By the late 1950s, increasingly restrictive state banning orders limited his ability to participate in po-litical activity. Luthuli is known as a staunch advocate of nonviolence, a moderate who never countenanced the ANC's armed resistance. But recently available archival documents and a rich vein of autobiographical accounts and oral interviews reveal that Luthuli, who rejected claims that he was a moderate, had a lesser-known, harder-edged activism. He eventually accepted armed self-defense against an apartheid state that he regarded as a relic or reinvention of Nazi-era fascism, engaged in virtual slavery and the literal imprisonment of a multitude of Africans.[1] Apartheid continued for decades after his tragic 1967 death on railway tracks in the isolated reserve of Groutville. Africa's first Nobel Peace Prize winner became a forgotten man, particularly outside South Africa.[2]

How did Albert Luthuli's many life experiences—as a Zulu, an African, an educator, a Christian, a government chief, a doting family man, and a sportsman—shape him as a person and a political leader? On the night of December 15, 1961, as Luthuli and his wife returned to South Africa five days after his Nobel acceptance, ANC members of a new military wing known as Umkhonto weSizwe (Spear of the Nation, or MK) set off the explosive charges that marked the start of their armed struggle.[3] The MK explosions raised doubts then and now: Was Luthuli a political contortionist, climbing the pedestal of peace while stooping to war? Had he been disingenuous to Nobel luminaries about his commitment to nonviolence? Or did Luthuli's trip to Norway give ANC renegades the opportunity to contravene his strategy of civil disobedience? Was he complicit in MK's incendiary debut? If so, was his nonviolence more pragmatic than principled, more situational than unshakeable? How did he react to the appeals of future

Nobel recipient Nelson Mandela, who wanted Luthuli's approval before destroying installations and training saboteurs? What relevance do his life and times have for today's South Africa and for the contemporary world? This biography aims to recover Luthuli from historical obscurity and highlight his key leadership of the ANC as it transformed into a mass antiapartheid movement and his revolutionary belief that apartheid South Africa could become one of the world's first truly multiracial democracies. Far from being a moderate, Luthuli was a revolutionary for his deep conviction that South Africa, founded on the bedrock of racial subordination and racial separation, could be a global model for a radical new form of multiracial democracy.

1

The Education of a
Zulu Christian

Albert John Mvumbi Luthuli was born around 1898 at the Seventh Day Adventist Solusi mission station in Bulawayo, Southern Rhodesia. His father, John, was an evangelist, teacher, interpreter, and goods transporter for missionaries and the British South Africa Company, then waging war against Mzilikazi and the Ndebele in what later resistance movements would come to know as the first Chimurenga, the 1896–97 African rebellions against Southern Rhodesian colonialism (the second Chimurenga was the guerrilla war that ended with the establishment of the independent state of Zimbabwe in 1980).[1] His mother, Nozililo Mtonya, had resided as a girl in the royal court of King Cetewayo before British forces conquered Zululand in 1879. The couple had three children, Alfred Nsusana, Mpangwa (who died at birth), and Albert, before John died, possibly during a malaria outbreak, when Albert was only six months old. Tending fifteen acres of land that John had previously bought, Nozililo, Alfred, and Albert remained in Southern Rhodesia until 1908, when they returned to

South Africa, moving to the Vryheid district in northern Natal, where Alfred became an interpreter for a Seventh Day Adventist mission. Because there were no schools in Vryheid for Albert to attend, Nozililo sent him to Groutville, Natal, a small community of mostly Christian peasant farmers attached to the local mission station of the American Board of Commissioners for Foreign Missions (ABM). The ABM was a Congregationalist enterprise that had begun its work in southern Africa in 1834. ABM missionary Aldin Grout founded the Umvoti mission station (the small town that grew up there was renamed Groutville after his death in 1894), where Albert's paternal grandparents, Ntaba ka Madunjini and Titisi Mthethwa, were his first Christian converts. Ntaba and Titisi were among the Africans who resisted incorporation into the expansive Zulu state founded by Shaka ka Senzengakhona. In 1860, the Umvoti mission community, known as the *abasemakholweni* (converted Christians), elected Ntaba as their chief, beginning a type of family tradition, as Ntaba's brother, son Martin, and grandson Albert also became elected chiefs, together comprising four of their first seven chiefs.[2]

The 1910 Union of South Africa consolidated white rule, immediately rooted in nineteenth-century land conquests by Dutch-descended whites known as Afrikaners, but particularly by the British, who subdued most Africans, including the large Xhosa and Zulu states, by the 1880s. The 1867 discovery of diamonds in Kimberley, soon controlled by the British Cape Colony, and in 1886, gold in the Transvaal, an Afrikaner-controlled state, led to the institution of the migrant labor system, which exploited Africans. By 1900, South Africa had become the world's leading producer of these minerals. Segregation laws designed to deny Africans citizenship rights began in the Cape Colony, before the establishment of South Africa, and continued with the 1892 Franchise and Ballot Act, which used financial and educational qualifications to limit the African vote, and the 1894 Glen Grey Act, which assigned areas to segregate Africans from whites. Such legislation began a segregationist onslaught that denied Africans the right to vote; condemned them, by "color-bar" laws, to the lowest-paying jobs; and provided them little judicial recourse to counter their systematic subordination. The British consolidated their political and economic control after they defeated the two Afrikaner republics, Transvaal and the Free State, in the South African War (1899–1902). Despite mutual dislike and distrust between many Afrikaners and British, these whites shared an even deeper disdain for the Africans, who made up about 70 percent of the population. The Union of South Africa became a self-governing dominion within the British Empire; Afrikaners, about 60 percent of the white population, exercised significant domestic political power. Africans were almost completely disenfranchised and were thus powerless to stop segregationist laws that maintained white supremacy. These laws included the Natives Land Act of 1913 and the Native Trust and Land Act of 1936, which limited

African landownership to less than 13 percent of South African territory. By restricting their abilities to own sufficient land for housing and to support the cattle holding and agricultural cultivation necessary to maintain economic independence, the laws forced them into labor tenancy and sharecropping on white farms.[3] The laws also accelerated African labor migration to urban areas, where migrants became subject to the Natives (Urban Areas) Act of 1923, which segregated them in squalid townships, declared them temporary workers instead of permanent urban residents, and restricted their movements with pass laws.

Nozililo sent Albert back to Groutville for schooling, where he lived in the orderly and deeply Christian household of his uncle Martin and his wife, who were also guardians to many other relatives and children. Martin was Groutville's first democratically elected chief, translator and interpreter for the Zulu royal house, secretary to the Zulu king Dinizulu, and a cofounder of both the Natal Native Congress in 1901 and the South African Native National Congress (later renamed the African National Congress) in 1912, groups that agitated for greater African political rights and land ownership. Serving until 1921, Martin provided Albert with a model for the Groutville chieftainship and an early exposure to African politics.[4] Albert also learned Zulu traditions and performed the typical duties of a Zulu child: herding cattle, weeding crops, fetching water, and building nighttime fires to keep the household warm—this last he did so well that Martin fondly recalled Albert's arrival as heralding the end of the household's chilly nights. As a herd boy, young Albert presumably would have learned stick fighting, as he carried his cattle switch (for fencing and parrying) in the presence of rivals. As segregationist laws restricted African life, stick fighting became an enduring vestige of precolonial exercise that primed boys for the ideals of manly dignity, *indoda enesithunzi*. Period ethnographies narrate bouts that adhered to ethical conduct, with opponents pausing to fix shields and withdrawing if an adversary fell (and therefore defaulted to his noncombatant identity). Competitors were exposed to serious injury, even death, which made disciplined restraint, *inkuliso*, the rule of combat. Boys were taught to prize self-defense and respect life, but also to project aggression to opponents (e.g., "Leli 'gwalana!" [This little coward!]).[5] These stick-fighting ethics bore some similarity to Luthuli's later reconciling of his nonviolent principles with the right to self-defense against life-threatening attackers. Luthuli later celebrated this male socialization and its historical accomplishment, Shaka's fusion of "bickering clans" into the "mightiest military force in Africa."[6]

When Alfred and Nozililo moved back to Groutville, Albert lived in a house built by his brother on a site where his grandparents had lived. He later praised the loving discipline of his mother, who gave him a "leathering" when he did not follow her instructions. She imparted the "strict" expectations of her Qwabe lineage, an *amadlozi*-worshiping "clan" with fiercely protective regiments. Albert attended the ABM mission school, Groutville Primary, where he passed Standard Four in 1914. Nozililo paid Albert's school fees by selling vegetables from her garden and taking in laundry for the white families in the nearby town of Stanger. He then went for two terms to Ohlange Institute, the school established by his admired mentor, the American-educated John Dube, the first SANNC president-general and founding editor of the African newspaper *Ilanga lase Natal*. After Ohlange, Luthuli attended Edendale, where Albert was one of many boys who briefly left the school as a protest against the disciplinary code requiring boys to carry stones from the river. Albert soon realized that this act of youthful impetuosity could have dire consequences; by leaving Edendale, the boys became subject to South African curfew and pass laws, risking arrest by the dreaded police. Martin promptly sent Albert back, after giving him the public thrashing required for readmission. Despite this brush with school authorities, Albert developed a love of teaching at Edendale, embarking on a two-year teacher-training course that resulted in a teaching certificate in 1917.[7]

After Edendale, he journeyed to the Natal Midlands, becoming the nineteen-year-old principal (and sole staff member) of a small school in Blaauwbosch. There, Luthuli became a Methodist lay minister though after leaving Blaauwbosch he returned to Congregationalism as a lay minister. Luthuli received a government scholarship to take the higher teachers' training course at Adams College in Amanzimtoti, where he earned his higher teacher's certificate in 1921.[8] Adams College was just beginning to employ Africans to train African teachers, and Luthuli, along with Z. K. Matthews, became one of the first African teachers there. Determined to bring education to as many young Africans as possible, Luthuli headed the Teachers' College at Adams, training future teachers and traveling by motorbike to teach at a number of surrounding schools. With Matthews, he also cofounded the African Teachers Association, a campus-based organization that sought higher wages.[9] He taught Zulu history, music, and literature, cofounding the Zulu Cultural and Language Society to steep younger generations in Zulu history and culture and to promote isiZulu as a medium for primary education. A passionate lover of music, Luthuli, along with his student Reuben Caluza—soon to win fame as a composer—founded the Adams College school of music in 1935 and led choirs renowned throughout Natal.[10] Luthuli conducted the Sunday church choir, gave well-received sermons, and, as a leader in the Adams branch of the Young Men's Christian Association (YMCA), interacted with African American YMCA missionary Max Yergan, who praised Luthuli for his role in expanding YMCA work.[11] Highly skilled at association football (i.e., soccer), Luthuli attended Adams football practices, coached football teams, and organized football leagues.[12]

Class photo, probably Adams College, c. 1920. Luthuli is seated in the first row, fifth from the right. (Luthuli Museum)

Luthuli courted Nokukhanya ka Maphita ka Bhengu Ndlokolo, the granddaughter of a Zulu chief, who had studied, then taught, at Adams. The two married in 1927, but, since Adams's regulations barred married female teachers, Nokukhanya then established the Luthuli family home back in Groutville. Thus, like so many Africans, the Luthulis lived apart, with Albert journeying to Groutville on some weekends and holidays. In Groutville, Nokukhanya learned Nozililo's successful farming methods to cultivate the family's small vegetable and sugarcane fields, selling enough produce to make her the family's primary breadwinner throughout their marriage.[13] The Luthulis had four daughters and three sons, born between 1929 and 1945: Hugh Bunyan Sulenkosi, Albertina, Thandeka Hilda Isabel, S'mangele Eleanor,

Thembekile Jane Elizabeth, Christian Madunjini, and Sibusiso Edgar.[14] The family lived in a simple two-bedroom house filled with religious statues, books, and Vladimir Tretchikoff prints. The household was deeply Christian, with regular Bible readings, prayers and hymns, and church attendance as a family. Luthuli was not a stereotypical authoritarian and distant patriarch; he enjoyed an equal partnership with Nokukhhanya and was a loving, attentive, and devoted father. Their eldest daughter, Albertina, recalled, "UBaba never imposed his status as family head upon us. Everybody had an equal opportunity to talk and no one was considered too young to have his views respected." Not surprisingly, the former teacher prized intellectual development, declaring, "Angivumi!" (I don't agree with you!) to initiate spirited debate in the household, and encouraged academic excellence, even returning letters written by his college-attending children with "grammar and spelling corrected in red ink."[15]

2

Chief of the People

Since 1933, Groutville residents had lobbied Luthuli to stand for election as their chief and oust the unpopular Chief Josiah Mqwebu, who had replaced Martin Luthuli in 1921. Initially, Albert was very reluctant, for he loved teaching and a chief's salary was only 20 percent of his Adams earnings. Some peers also rejected the notion that Luthuli, one of the very first African teachers at Adams, would abandon this high-status profession that ostensibly prepared young Africans for modern society to accept a putatively backward "traditional" chieftainship controlled and manipulated by the state.[1] But by December 1935, he and Nokukhanya finally answered the call, believing that "the voice of the people comes from God."

While rejoicing that they could now live together while raising their children, the couple knew that government chiefs like Luthuli were in a difficult, contradictory position, charged simultaneously with representing the interests of their people and administering unjust and unpopular government policies. Some chiefs used state backing to rule as tyrants while enriching themselves by laying claim to land, charging dubious fees, and accepting bribes for settling disputes. After winning Groutville's democratic elections for the chieftainship in December 1935 and being installed as chief in January 1936, Chief Luthuli, though now earning considerably less money, scorned such extortionist measures—though his children periodically complained about their spartan lifestyle. Practicing *Ubuntu*, a concept that recognized the humanity and interdependence of all people, he governed with an inclusive democratic spirit, personal warmth, integrity, empathy, and judicious wisdom. Luthuli understood Zulu traditional governance as democratic, with chiefs legally bound to rule according to traditional customs, remaining responsive to the needs and desires of their people.

Though Groutville was a largely Christian community, Africans there respected the Zulu royal house, proclaiming, "Our doors face in the direction of Zululand!" Accordingly, Luthuli made obligatory visits to the Zulu royal capital in Ulundi, meeting with other chiefs and prominent elders and reveling in Zulu and court rituals that confirmed for him that he was no "Black Englishman," since Zulu-ness was "in my blood."[2] His Congregationalist upbringing enhanced this democratic ethos as Luthuli worked with his *induna*—childhood friend and best man Robbins Guma—and a council of *amakholwa* (another term for converted Christians) and *amabhinca* (traditionalist) elders on judicial matters, reveling in the hard work of finding reconciliation

Congregationalist minister Posselt Gumede (*left*) and first ANC president John Dube (*right*) with Albert Luthuli (*center*) at Inanda Seminary, 1936. (Mwelela Cele, Campbell Collections of the University of KwaZulu-Natal)

and compromise with oppositional parties.[3] He also included women, regarded as legal and social minors, in democratic consultations and facilitated their economic advancement by disregarding government prohibitions on their beer brewing and selling and their operation of unlicensed bars known as shebeens.[4] Luthuli was a chief of and by, not above, his people, prominently leading the festive dancing and singing at community feasts. One community member remembered Luthuli as a "man of the people [who] had a very strong influence over the community. He was a people's chief."[5]

Chief Luthuli nurtured the ideal of community to mitigate against the 1913 and 1936 Land Acts, which entrenched black dislocation and impoverishment. The Land Acts were part of the structural violence of segregation nationwide, further eviscerating African landownership and increasing grinding poverty in overcrowded reserves while forcing extensive labor migration to urban areas, which separated families and furthered social disintegration and dislocation. Luthuli later noted the disparity of whites claiming to need 375 acres per person to live comfortably while African *families* had only 6 acres, leading to soil exhaustion, lack of adequate grazing ground for cattle, and little heritable land for grown African children to economically sustain themselves and their families. He railed against the "land rehabilitation" schemes, which forced Africans to sell "surplus" cattle at reduced rates to white farmers who had comparatively plentiful land to absorb additional cattle and accrue more wealth. "Your solution is to take our cattle away today because you took our land yesterday," Luthuli charged, telling unmoved state officials that cattle were cherished possessions and a meaningful source of wealth for Africans; forcing them to sell cattle represented a deep economic and psychic violence against his people.[6] Particularly in Natal, the government's 1936 Sugar Act, in attempting to keep sugar prices high by limiting production, disproportionately hurt African sugar-cane planters, who, in careful estimates Luthuli presented, lived substantially below the poverty line. Unlike white sugarcane farmers, African farmers held insufficient land, without legal title, and thus by law could not use their land as security on short-term loans to buy adequate machinery and fertilizer, thus offsetting the costs of planting, harvesting, and transporting sugar to the mills. As African migrant laborers left impoverished rural areas for work in the cities, some could not find work and became "redundant" urban workers, who then found themselves "deported" back to these same rural areas they had been forced to leave: a never-ending shuttle.

But state officials, including arrogant, culturally ignorant, and ineffective "agricultural demonstrators," insisted that African poverty was due not to inadequate land but to supposedly inefficient African agricultural techniques. Luthuli's chieftainship uniquely positioned him to observe the fallacy of state logic and the deepening poverty of the once-prosperous Groutville community and the tangible negative effects of African disfranchisement, onerous taxation without representation, land scarcity, and economic insecurity.[7] He immediately revived the Groutville Bantu Cane Growers' Association, a group of about two hundred small-scale cane growers (including himself) that successfully lobbied the millers to advance monies that would allow African farmers to meet upfront production costs. He also chaired the Natal and Zululand Bantu Cane Growers' Association, bringing nearly all African sugarcane producers into one union. His tour of America in 1948 enabled him to procure a tractor that helped boost agricultural production by local farmers, some of whom thus increased their margins enough to educate their children.[8] The African intellectual Jordan Ngubane, who studied at Adams when Luthuli taught there and later became Luthuli's personal secretary and political ally, credited the chief with promoting economic development, increasing agricultural efficiency, sending more youth to schools and universities, and inspiring an optimism that belied the increasing hardships caused by government land policies.[9]

Into Politics

Luthuli joined the ANC in 1944, partially out of respect for the recently deceased Natal ANC president John Dube. ANC president Dr. Alfred Xuma had reinvigorated an organization virtually dead in the 1930s. He used his own resources to pay prior debts and finance new initiatives, established new branches, and facilitated the formation of the ANC Women's League (1943) and the ANC Youth League (1944). Former Luthuli student Anton Lembede was the most influential Youth League leader. Before his untimely death in 1947, he influenced a young cadre of future national leaders including Walter Sisulu, Nelson Mandela, A. P. Mda, and Oliver Tambo to adopt a more confrontational posture toward white supremacy. The Atlantic Charter, issued in August 1941 by U.S. president Franklin Roosevelt and British prime minister Winston Churchill, defined British and American aims during World War II and their postwar aspirations. It declared, among other things, the right of all people to self-determination and the restoration of self-government. But Churchill and South African prime minister Jan Smuts claimed that self-determination applied only to countries occupied by fascist powers, not to European colonial possessions and South Africa. Thus, Luthuli and other Africans felt that support for Smuts's South Africa in the wider war against Hitler's Germany represented no more than a choice between white supremacist regimes, a "local master race versus the foreign one."[10] In 1943, accordingly, the ANC published *African Claims*, demanding for African self-determination, including a bill of rights, racial equality, universal suffrage, and nonracial citizenship for blacks in southern Africa.[11]

In 1946, Luthuli assumed councilor duties in the Native Representative Council (NRC), an advisory body to the government. Luthuli reiterated the demands made in *African Claims* and continued his longstanding complaints about inadequate African land, comments that enraged the white NRC chairman. With the support of other councilors, Luthuli protested the state's use of coercive force to suppress a massive African mineworkers' strike, condemning "the reactionary character of the Union Native Policy," which exposed the "government's post war continuation of a policy of fascism which is the antithesis of the letter and the spirit of the Atlantic Charter and the United Nations Charter." The government, he continued, was "impenetrably deaf" to African groans of pain in response to oppressive segregationist measures.[12] Luthuli would say later that the NRC was a "toy telephone" requiring him to "shout a little louder" to no one, and African councilors then adjourned in protest. The NRC never met again, and the government formally dissolved it in 1952.[13]

In 1947, Dr. Xuma and South African Indian Congress (SAIC) leaders Dr. Yusuf Dadoo and Dr. G. M. Naicker signed the "Doctors Pact," pledging to fight together against South Africa's racial policies, including at the newly founded United Nations (UN). Ironically, as Nazi-inspired apartheid leaders would soon rule South Africa, the UN's Universal Declaration of Human Rights exemplified an international human rights discourse that included racial equality, a partial reaction to the genocidal policies of Nazi Germany. Tellingly, South Africa abstained from the vote that approved the Human Rights Declaration. Gandhi, whose *satyagraha* campaigns while he was in South Africa between 1893 and 1914 set the course for his later successes in India, warned South Africa of its dangerous path: "the future is surely not with the so-called white races if they keep themselves in purdah. The attitude of unreason will mean a third war which sane people should avoid. Political cooperation among all the exploited races in South Africa can only result in mutual goodwill, if it is wisely directed and based on truth and non-violence."[14]

The unexpected victory of the National Party in May 1948 made apartheid official state policy until 1994. Founded in 1933 by Dutch Reformed Church (DRC) minister and newspaper editor Daniel François Malan, the National Party was the political beneficiary of a resurgent Afrikaner ethno-nationalism that sought economic advancement, cultural autonomy, and explicit political measures to ensure Afrikaner power and identity to counter British political and economic dominance and African numerical superiority. Many pro-Nazi Afrikaners, including future apartheid prime ministers Johannes Strydom and John Vorster, had opposed South African military and economic contributions to the Allied cause against Hitler's Germany, engaging in seditious activities that resulted in their detention during the war. As Africans and poor Afrikaners competed with each other for living space and jobs in a rapidly expanding manufacturing sector producing war materiel, Afrikaner nationalists complained of "swamping" by an African urban population that had doubled to 1.4 million in the interwar years. By 1946, there were 2.2 million urban-based Africans living in cities supposedly reserved for white permanent residence, and their growing militancy was exemplified in strikes, boycotts, and demands for better living and working conditions. Also, the close proximity of working-class Africans and Afrikaners renewed fears of racial mixing and prompted calls for policies that would ensure Afrikaner racial separation and preservation. Increasingly, Afrikaner intellectuals posited apartheid as a permanent solution for "the purity of our blood and . . . our unadulterated European racial survival."[15] The governing United Party of Prime Minister Jan Smuts, South Africa's most prominent political figure, who also helped found the League of Nations and its successor the UN, had trounced the Nationalists in the previous 1943 election. In 1948, the United Party won the popular vote again, but because of greater electoral weight given to rural districts, which voted disproportionately for the Nationalists, and an alliance with a smaller Afrikaner-based Party, the Nationalists squeezed out an improbable victory. The surprised Malan, now faced with the unexpected task of converting apartheid from electoral slogan to concrete government policy, nevertheless hastened to hail the victory as divinely ordained.[16]

The Global Color Line

South Africa was part of the global hegemony of powerful white states and individuals exemplified by European

33

colonialism in Africa, Asia, and the Caribbean and continuing racial subordination in the United States. In June 1948, Luthuli traveled to the United States for seven months, during which he addressed churches, civic groups, youth groups, and others about the progress of Natal American Board missions, African rural development, and racial reconciliation.[17] This was not his first overseas trip; in 1938, the chief had traveled to Madras, India, as part of an interracial Christian delegation to an international missionary conference. Despite the fact that South African segregation traveled outside its borders—white delegates traveled first class and the four Africans second class—Luthuli toured India and Ceylon (present-day Sri Lanka), met Indian, Japanese, Chinese, and African Christian leaders, and returned "with wider sympathies and wider horizons."[18] Luthuli's tour of the United States took place during the 1948 presidential election, when President Harry Truman put forth a mild but virtually unprecedented civil rights agenda that sparked the "Dixiecrat" revolt of southern segregationists. Luthuli hoped that African Americans, who, unlike black South Africans, had constitutional rights, would ultimately triumph over Jim Crow practices and that the United States would be a positive model of multiracial democracy for his own country.

Suspecting that the South African government was monitoring him closely, Luthuli toured the South on Jim Crow trains to visit historically black universities—Howard, Atlanta, Tuskegee, and Virginia State—

Albert Luthuli during his tour of the United States, 1948.
(Luthuli Museum)

remarking, "I have such a great desire to visit my people in the South that I would have been awfully disappointed to return to Africa without doing so." At Howard, Luthuli lectured on African history, met African students, marveled at the library's vast book collection on Africa, and was hosted by members of Washington's bustling, upwardly mobile black communities. During his lectures he explained enduring values of Zulu traditional society, Zulu religious concepts, and Zulus' respect for law and order.[19] In the wake of Gandhi's assassination, Luthuli, who would later use Gandhian methods in the ANC's antiapartheid campaigns, also lectured to the Mahatma Gandhi Memorial Society about Gandhi's development of his nonviolent philosophy and strategy of satyagraha.[20] While at Virginia State and Tuskegee, Luthuli visited black-owned and operated dairies, among other rural-based development and school projects. He discussed sustainable agricultural methods with successful black farmers and initiated conversations with rural parents and children about the quality of their education. His Virginia State host, Dr. Samuel Gandy, described Luthuli as "vigorous, hale and hearty . . . a living symbol of vitality" who was "easy to meet and know and brought no distinctions with him." His visit sparked an "awakening on campus relative to Africa and an eagerness on the part of students to know more about this great continent."[21] At Tuskegee, Luthuli personally witnessed the industrial education model championed by the American-educated South African agricultural official C. T. Loram—a model that would be foundational to South Africa's Bantu education system—concluding that the "manual crafts ... do not seem to me to justify university degrees."[22]

Jim Crow was ubiquitous. Howard, the mecca of black education and the educational pillar of an upwardly mobile black elite, was in the nation's capital, the Jim Crow city of Washington, D.C. In Virginia, a restaurant did not allow Luthuli and Gandy to eat on the premises. Upon discovering Luthuli's South African origins, the owner effectively declared Luthuli an "honorary white," telling him he could stay, but not Gandy, whereupon the exasperated men left in disgust. Luthuli remarked that this southern tour had a profound effect on him, allowing him to "see South African issues more sharply, and in a different and larger perspective."[23] Luthuli's American tour reminded him of the transnational nature of white supremacy: "those moments—a door closed in one's face, a restaurant where a cup of coffee has been refused—that jolt the black man back to the realization that, almost everywhere he travels, race prejudice will not let him be at home in the world."[24] Luthuli heard stories from African Americans insulted by long-time prime minister Jan Smuts, who in 1929 had told American blacks that Africans "were the most patient of all animals, next to the ass."[25] Luthuli left America in February 1949 having felt the sting of American Jim Crow but also encouraged by African American progress against long odds.

When Luthuli returned to South Africa, the National Party, keenly aware that their slender electoral victory could be overturned in the next elections, was already moving to translate apartheid from a provocative electoral slogan into a comprehensive and ambitious social engineering political program that would ensure ethnic Afrikaner advancement and white racial supremacy. The Prohibition of Mixed Marriages Act (1949) and the Immorality Act (1950) outlawed marriage and sexual relations between whites and other racial groups. The Suppression of Communism Act (1950) stifled political dissent by defining communism broadly to include any resistance to the apartheid state. The Population Registration Act (1950) divided South Africa's inhabitants into four racial groups, Africans, Coloureds, Asiatics, and Whites—and on this basis the National Party set out to create racially differentiated citizens and subjects in their "own" residential areas, with different employment, educational, political, economic, and social rights. The Group Areas Act (1950) extended government powers to create racially separate residential zones, including the forcible removal of people to create racially homogeneous areas. In Luthuli's view, the apartheid regime and its white supporters had pirated the land, wealth, and government. More particularly, it had claimed ownership of the African majority, virtually enslaving them through apartheid laws. Africans were the "livestock which went with the estate, objects rather than subjects," political footballs tossed about by the Nationalists and their white parliamentary rivals.[26]

At the December 1948 conference, ANC Youth Leaguers such as A. P. Mda, Walter Sisulu, Nelson Mandela, and Oliver Tambo argued that the advent of the new apartheid regime forced the ANC to move beyond strictly constitutional methods. They proposed a Program of Action that would consist of civil disobedience tactics, including strikes and boycotts. Before the December 1949 ANC annual conference, they challenged Xuma to move beyond strictly constitutional measures to fight apartheid, but he refused to commit himself to the Program of Action. Inspired partially by Kwame Nkrumah's direct-action anticolonial stance in the Gold Coast, the Youth Leaguers effectively seized power within the ANC at the 1949 conference, as delegates voted to adopt the Program of Action. Delegates also voted for the Youth League's candidate for president-general, Dr. James Moroka, who defeated the chastened Xuma. Sisulu became ANC secretary-general, and six Youth Leaguers joined the National Executive.[27]

Luthuli would lead the execution of the Program of Action in Natal. Allison Wessels George (A. W. G.) Champion, who regarded the provincial Natal ANC as his personal fiefdom and felt no obligation to enact national ANC initiatives, also opposed the Program of Action. After initial reservations about African-Indian collaboration after the January 1949 Durban riots, in which some Africans, frustrated by the perceived arrogance and discrimination of Indians toward them, attacked Indians, Luthuli participated in joint-action campaigns with the Indian Congresses. This included a one-day strike on May 1, 1950, in which the South African police killed at least eighteen unarmed, non-violent protesters, and a multiracial one-day stay at home on June 26, 1950, to protest the Group Areas Act and the Suppression of Communism Act. Luthuli resigned from Champion's executive committee in protest of his dictatorial control of the Natal ANC, his opposition to the Program of Action, and his general resistance to national ANC centralization efforts.[28] ANC leaders in Transvaal and Natal, particularly influential Youth League leaders M. B. Yengwa and Wilson Conco, and Jordan Ngubane, editor of the African newspaper *Inkundla ya Bantu*, persuaded Luthuli to stand as Natal ANC president at the 1951 Natal ANC conference.[29] As Yengwa, who became Luthuli's close ally as Natal ANC secretary and NEC member, noted, "Mr. Champion was not prepared to cooperate with the Indians, but . . . we argued that we have no alternative but to work with the Indians, that we are fighting the same enemy."[30] On May 3, 1951, Luthuli became Natal ANC president, defeating Champion in a contentious, raucous election. Though the embittered Champion became a longtime antagonist, Luthuli's victory facilitated greater cooperation with the Transvaal-based national ANC and set the stage for Natal's participation in the iconic Defiance Campaign.[31]

3

The Nonviolent, Multiracial
Politics of Defiance

The Defiance Campaign

Luthuli became a national political figure during the iconic 1952 Defiance Campaign, a multiracial mobilization to resist apartheid led by the ANC, the SAIC, and the Coloured Peoples Convention (CPC). Luthuli led protests in Natal against the Pass Laws, Group Areas Act, the Separate Voters' Representation Act, the Suppression of Communism Act, and the Bantu Authorities Act. The campaign modeled itself on Gandhi's nonviolent civil disobedience strategy, which helped win India's independence from Great Britain, and the mid-1940s Indian passive resistance campaigns against the so called Ghetto Act, which disenfranchised Indians and restricted their land ownership.[1] Luthuli endorsed Gandhi's satyagraha as an "active non-violence" that he felt had the power to change individual lives, mobilize the masses, and end apartheid. "We have declared to the world that we do not mean to use violence in furtherance of our cause. We will always follow the path of peace and non-violence in our legitimate demands for freedom."[2] In April 1952, he gathered Natal ANC members to reaffirm their commitment to the Defiance Campaign, a pivotal moment that his close friend M. B. Yengwa remembered reflected his unprecedented willingness to defy government laws despite being a government-paid chief.[3]

Luthuli's role as a staff officer was not to be arrested and go to jail, but to tour Natal to organize the campaign. With his rich baritone voice, he led crowds singing freedom songs. The Natal Campaign began in August 1952 as a joint ANC-SAIC endeavor, marking the first large-scale cooperation between Africans, Indians, and other racial groups in the province. Luthuli rallied thousands of people as Africans and Indians defied segregation practices in public facilities and Africans defied curfew laws in Durban.[4] Over nine thousand people of all races went to jail for defying apartheid laws, and the prisons resounded with their freedom songs. The Defiance Campaign lived up to its name, but it was never going to bring the walls—or the laws—of apartheid tumbling down. Instead, the government used brute force to eliminate all "subversive" activity, soon to be defined yet more comprehensively.[5] Nevertheless, the Defiance Campaign led to a dramatic increase in ANC membership (from an estimated twenty-five thousand in 1951 to one hundred thousand at the

Luthuli signing up volunteers for the Defiance Campaign, 1952. (Luthuli Museum)

end of the campaign). It also facilitated the Congress Alliance, a broad antiapartheid front of independent multiracial, multi-ideological organizations that sought to end apartheid. If the Defiance Campaign did not end apartheid, it prepared its downfall by transforming the character and nature of the antiapartheid struggle.

This was particularly significant in Natal, where memories of the Durban riots reinforced mutual suspicion and hostility between Indians and Africans. Even Gandhi had exhibited racial antagonism toward Africans, and his son, Manilal, who had remained in Natal, had previously referred to Africans' "savage instinct" and doubted their ability to attain and maintain the spiritual and personal discipline to utilize satyagraha techniques.[6] But Luthuli's inclusive leadership style, open admiration for Gandhi's satyagraha methods, and close relationships with Indian leaders, including Manilal, facilitated unprecedented levels of cooperation between Africans and Indians.[7] Luthuli was a crucial influence on future Indian Congressites such as the antiapartheid activist Kader Asmal, who remembered, "I met him on a number of occasions in the late 1940s and early 1950s when he knocked on doors in my home town of Stanger looking for support. His non-racialism and his commitment to freedom and democracy made an indelible impression on me. Albert Luthuli was one of the most important influences leading me into the politics of liberation."[8] Luthuli's multiracial stance allayed the suspicions of Indians and whites harbored by ANC activists like Dorothy Nyembe, who remembered how "Chief Luthuli taught us that every person born in this country had a right to stay and be free, whether he is Indian, African or white. We fought side by side."[9]

From Government Chief to ANC President

By August 1952, government officials had concluded—not surprisingly—that Luthuli's Defiance Campaign activity conflicted with his chiefly duties to administer and enforce government laws. Summoning Luthuli to

Pretoria, Secretary of Native Affairs Dr. W. W. M. Eiselen ordered Luthuli to resign from either the ANC or the chieftaincy. When, after two months, Luthuli refused to choose, the government stripped him of his chieftainship, which included benefits such as paid school fees for his children. But Luthuli insisted, "a chief is primarily a servant of his people . . . not a local agent of the Government. . . . Why shouldn't [Africans] assist this organization which fights for the welfare of the black man?"[10] Luthuli lamented,

> who will deny that thirty years of my life have been spent knocking in vain, patiently, moderately at a closed and barred door? What have been the fruits of my many years of moderation? . . .
>
> . . . Has there been any reciprocal tolerance or moderation from the Government, be it Nationalist or United Party? No! No! On the contrary, the past 30 years have seen the greatest number of laws restricting our rights and progress until today, we have reached a stage where we have almost no rights at all: no adequate land for our occupation; our only asset, cattle, dwindling; no security of home ownership; no decent and remunerative employment; more restriction of freedom of movement by the pass laws, curfew regulations, influx control measures; in short we have witnessed in these years an intensification of our subjection to ensure and protect white supremacy.[11]

Luthuli fought apartheid on political *and* theological grounds, regarding Christianity as a stirring social gospel of justice, freedom, and equality and Jesus as the champion of the dispossessed who had died on the cross for all of humanity, not just whites. Luthuli argued that all Christians should fight for social justice, his politics reflecting his own understanding of Christianity: "I am in Congress precisely because I am a Christian. My Christian belief about human society must find expression here and now. . . . My own urge, because I am a Christian, is to get into the thick of the struggle with other Christians, taking my Christianity with me and praying that it may be used to influence for good the character of the resistance."[12] Thus, he criticized the many whites, especially within the Afrikaner Dutch Reformed Church (DRC), who used Christianity to justify white supremacy, relying on the Calvinist doctrine of an "elect" in claiming divine sanction to rule South Africa as a supreme and separate population over blacks.[13] DRC religious leaders championed apartheid as a divinely ordained, comprehensive social engineering program that would create societal harmony through rigorous political, socioeconomic, and physical separation, thereby eliminating the supposed evils of racial egalitarianism.[14] Despite the Christian principle of an "equality of believers" regardless of race, proapartheid self-professed "Christians" argued that in racial matters "all earthly distinctions remain."[15] For Luthuli, apartheid was a violation of God's law, "contrary to the plan and purpose of God our Creator, who created all men equal."[16]

At the ANC annual conference in December 1952, ANC delegates including Walter Sisulu, impressed by Luthuli's "defiance of the government," elected him president over Moroka, who had hired his own lawyer and disavowed Congress policies in court after being arrested for Defiance Campaign involvement.[17] Taking the mantle of an organization that had just had fifty-two leaders banned, twenty leaders, including Moroka, and over eight thousand volunteers convicted for Defiance Campaign activities, Luthuli immediately visited national ANC branches countrywide. In the Eastern Cape's Port Elizabeth, twenty-five thousand people came to hear him demand, "Vula Malan thina siya qonqotha" (Open the door, Malan, we are knocking!"), and sang, "Malan o tshohilole 'muso oa hae. Luthuli phakisa onke'muso!" (Malan has taken fright, make haste, Luthuli, and form a new government!).[18] At home, Nokukhanya vetted Albert's speeches as they hosted visiting ANC members and friends such as Nelson Mandela, Mangosuthu Buthelezi, and other visitors, who, showing customary Zulu respect before entering someone's home, addressed Luthuli by his clan name: "O! Madlanduna, Mashisha Sikhulekile Ekhaya."[19]

The Violence of the Apartheid State

In response to the Defiance Campaign, apartheid South Africa evolved further toward a police state, with bans that forced Eastern Cape ANC branches underground and police raids of homes and workplaces of campaign leaders, including Luthuli, to confiscate Defiance Campaign documents, membership cards, organizational papers, and files. With the introduction of the Public Safety Act and the Criminal Law Amendment Act in 1953, the state could proclaim states of emergency; suspend the rule of law; expand its arrest powers; place restrictions on freedoms of assembly, speech, and movement; and ban the words and images of activists. The white electorate seemingly approved of these repressive tactics, as the Nationalists gained twenty-four parliamentary seats in the April 1953 elections. The judiciary was another instrument of domination; in addition to the December 1952 convictions of ANC leaders, the state convicted fifteen Defiance Campaign leaders in Port Elizabeth in 1953 of contravening the Suppression of Communism Act.[20]

Luthuli condemned the National Party's "fascist dictatorship" and the "anti-Defiance Acts," which evoked the "unfortunate Medieval Dark Ages." Lamenting the apartheid "chain of bondage" that left Africans "prisoners in their own castle," he nevertheless celebrated the significant domestic and international support for the Defiance Campaign's fight for democracy and the "fundamental human rights of freedom of speech, association and movement," which would achieve "racial harmony in the Union," bringing South Africa into modern civilization.[21] He felt that only an inclusive African nationalism, expressed by a broad ANC-led multiracial coalition, could defeat apartheid and create a postapartheid, inclusive, egalitarian, equitable, and democratic South Africa. In sharp contrast to National Party leaders, who cast apartheid as the solution to the supposed problem of multiracial societies and an international model for other racially mixed countries, Luthuli reconciled the seemingly oppositional political claims of national unity and racial diversity. "I personally believe that here in South Africa, with all our diversities of color and race, we will show the world a new pattern of democracy. . . . We can build a homogeneous South Africa on the basis not of colour but of human values."[22] His inclusive nationalism asserted the primacy of African claims based on their indigenous status, their numerical majority, and the longevity of their struggle. But unlike the Lembedist exclusive African nationalism of the 1940s, Luthuli did not present whites and other racial groups as foreigners, but as permanently settled South Africans.

Luthuli's previous coordination with Natal Indian Congress (NIC) president G. M. Naicker, vice president J. N. Singh, and future NIC vice president Ismail Meer during the Defiance Campaign lessened lingering post–Durban Riots African-Indian tensions.[23] As ANC president, Luthuli built "a political alliance based on a common, genuine spirit of friendship between our respective communities." He organized a mass rally of several thousand people in Durban to protest the lack of educational facilities and opportunities for African and Indian children before police tossed him in jail.[24] Undeterred, Luthuli presided over an ANC-NIC joint meeting in Durban to protest the Public Safety Bill and the Criminal Law Amendment Bill.[25] Luthuli and Naicker issued a joint ANC-NIC protest statement from the "voteless and democratic peoples of South Africa," who condemned Nationalist Party apartheid policies, and the ANC invited the NIC to join a planned stay-at-home during the national elections in April 1953, utilizing the same nonviolent principles used recently by bus boycotters in Johannesburg.[26] Amidst government threats to repatriate Indian-descended South Africans back to India, Luthuli often addressed NIC conferences, expertly critiquing the Natives Land Acts, the Urban Areas Act, and the Group Areas Act as the primary cause, respectively, of the chronic landlessness, lack of urban property, and general insecurity of Africans in South Africa, which he compared to Nazi Germany. Naicker followed the call of Luthuli, "our President-General," to commemorate June 26, 1953—the third anniversary of the murder of peacefully striking Africans by government forces, and the first anniversary of the Defiance Campaign—as Freedom Day, and urged all NIC branches to participate.[27] This day

New ANC president Luthuli gives the "Africa" sign to delegates at the December 1953 ANC national conference in Queenstown. Luthuli attended this conference despite his banning orders. (Bailey's African History Archives, photograph by Bob Gosani)

became a sacred day of service and rededicated commitment to the freedom struggle in South Africa.[28]

In May 1953, the regime banned Luthuli, claiming that his political activities promoted "feelings of hostility in the Union of South Africa between the European inhabitants and the non-European section of the inhabitants of the Union."[29] The ban confined Luthuli to Groutville and the surrounding Stanger district and prohibited him from entering major South African cities, attending political meetings or public gatherings (defined as five or more people together in the same space), making speeches, and visiting ANC branches. With Special Branch police increasing their raids of Luthuli's house in search of "subversive" documents, Minister of Native Affairs Hendrik Verwoerd denounced him in Parliament as a dangerous radical championing equal rights, and Prime Minister Malan called the ANC a terrorist group "on the pattern of the Mau Mau" in Kenya.[30] South African authorities lamented that Luthuli, previously regarded as a "good Native[,] . . . had now been bought by the Indians and was definitely under Communist influence."[31]

Escalating state and popular violence marked the 1950s. Luthuli and others advocating Gandhian nonviolent civil disobedience clashed with younger militants willing to consider armed self-defense in debates that surged to the fore during the Defiance Campaign. On November 9, 1952, the lay minister Luthuli delivered a sermon titled "Christian Life: A Constant Venture," the basis for his manifesto "The Road to Freedom Is Via the Cross," which compared apartheid South Africa to Nazi Germany and affirmed nonviolent struggle.[32] Luthuli could not know that this very day would become known as Black Sunday, when police fired on ANC supporters praying with Defiance Campaigners in East London's Duncan Village. Africans responded by burning government facilities; in the chaos, a few whites died, but militarized police killed two hundred–plus Duncan Villagers, according to estimates.[33] The carnage raised doubts within the ANC about the efficacy of civil disobedience. The Criminal Law Amendment and Public Safety Act expanded government powers to crush antiapartheid dissent. Mandela, Sisulu, Mda, and the ANC Executive discussed armed self-defense and critiqued what seemed to be a "useless" nonviolent strategy, but for the time being they decided "it was politically wise" to maintain a nonviolent posture.[34] Pivotal ANC leader Govan Mbeki encountered Mpondoland Africans who argued to him that whites' superior firepower had facilitated their nineteenth-century conquests over Africans, who would not regain their independence until they had sufficient arms. Thus, the Defiance Campaign's nonviolent tactics would not overthrow the state, but only "tickle the beard of the Boers."[35] In 1953, Sisulu embarked on a months-long tour of Romania, the Soviet Union, and China, whose armed struggle was inspirational to some South Africans, raising the possibility of armed self-defense with Chinese and Soviet officials.[36] Sisulu later told Luthuli of other "revolutionary" stirrings, prompting the president-general to later admit that "non-Whites" appeared "ready at any time to change the non-violent aspect of our movement, to violence."[37] Luthuli made public assurances that "we do not mean to use violence in furtherance of our cause."[38] But beyond the public glare, he was also articulating militant thoughts. In a 1953 letter to his friend ANC leader Z. K. Matthews, Luthuli confided that he hankered to "fight for freedom" as American abolitionists once did, evoking the 1859 revolt of John Brown (and his black freedom fighters), who in killing slaveholders on the eve of the U.S. Civil War advanced the Law of the Israelites (Hebrews 9:22): "without the shedding of blood there is no remission of sin."[39]

From the beginning of his presidency, Luthuli reckoned with concerns about undue communist influence in the ANC. Jordan Ngubane had believed that Luthuli was the right person to build the ANC and its African nationalism and execute its Program of Action along with "Gandhian satyagraha" nonviolent methods instead of "Marxian violence." He was not averse to the ANC building multiracial links, with allies occupying a secondary, supportive role in the struggle. But Ngubane cautioned Luthuli about the potentially negative impact of the ANC left wing, claiming that communists and leftists could impose their ideologies on African peoples who ultimately wanted African nationalism. He also claimed that there were "several communists among the non-European leaders, notably in the Transvaal, whose adherence to non-violence is purely temporary and tactical," and feared that nonviolence could eventually be discredited in favor of armed self-defense.[40] Ngubane claimed that Sisulu had not received NEC authority to undertake his overseas trip and charged that the communists had "sabotaged" the ANC, sponsoring trips abroad not authorized by Luthuli.[41] Luthuli countered that African nationalism and the nonviolent passive resistance strategies of the Indian National Congress of India—not communism—were the dominant ideas and methods of the ANC, and that these had increased the organization's militancy. He noted that Sisulu's recent trips to communist countries were part of a personal invitation, not sponsored by the ANC. He also said that the ANC, "in general, follows the foreign policy of Nehru which sought neutrality and was willing to accept assistance in freedom struggles from whomever offered it."[42] An American pacifist visiting South Africa in 1953, Douglas Steere, wondered if ANC members supported Luthuli. Steere pondered the president-general's "position in the Congress ... surrounded by men ... [who] do not share his convictions and principles.... Whether Luthuli can hold this group together and mold them into a strong group on sound lines is to be seen." Steere claimed that there were "more bitter direct-action people" that sought to "carry off the Congress in the end."[43]

Setbacks: Sophiatown and the Bantu Education Act

Just before Luthuli was to address residents from Sophiatown, a Johannesburg community of black property holders facing forced removals, state officials served him with new banning orders restricting him to a twenty-mile radius of Groutville and forbidding him to speak in either urban or rural towns.[44] Despite the ANC's determination to fight against the forced removals, the government relocated Sophiatown residents to the desolate Meadowlands township, and they gloated over their victory by renaming Sophiatown Triomf ("triumph" in Afrikaans). Forced removals prompted additional calls for armed self-defense.

Enraged ANC vice president Nelson Mandela vowed to "overthrow a white minority regime bent on . . . power at any cost," declaring nonviolence to be "an ineffective weapon."[45] ANC and SACP member Flag Boshielo also contemplated armed self-defense, particularly studying the Mau Mau armed revolt.[46] At a 1954 ANC rally in Port Elizabeth, the crowd chanted, "Dien Bien Phu" to celebrate the Viet Minh victory there that ended French colonialism.[47]

But there were yet more apartheid laws. The 1953 Bantu Education Act mandated government-controlled separate and unequal African education that would train African children to accept their permanent subordination, coordinating with other apartheid laws to reinforce existing master-servant relations. Designed to wrest control of African education from mission schools like Luthuli's Adams, the act was the culmination of Loram's American-inspired industrial education model for Africans to "develop along their own lines." Minister of Native Affairs Hendrik Verwoerd anticipated his eventual control of African education, when "Natives will be taught from childhood to realize that equality with the Europeans is not for them."[48] Luthuli condemned Bantu education as a political tool to deny Africans citizenship and socioeconomic advancement, instead focusing on narrow ethnic tribalism, with its emphasis on specific ethnic schools, cultural training, and the use of vernacular languages to isolate young Africans from the cultural heritage of Western civilization.[49] He urged teachers to teach children the truth of African dispossession and to reject the pernicious stereotypes of African inferiority that undergirded apartheid.[50] He later wrote that Bantu education was the government response to the mission-trained class of African teachers, ministers, lawyers, doctors, and other professionals, which was vocally demanding full political, economic, and social citizenship; instead, Africans were to be trained to accept their permanent inferiority. "It is a tool in the hands of the white master for the more effective reduction and control of the black servant."[51] Luthuli also noted that the Bantu education plan was woefully underfunded, with a permanently frozen state contribution of 6.5 million pounds; given the rapidly growing African school-age population, parents would have to pay increasingly more to subsidize their children's education.[52]

The ANC annual conference in December 1954 planned a nationwide permanent school boycott to begin on April 1, 1955, the day of the government takeover of schools. However, various setbacks and strategic weaknesses undermined the ANC's bold attempt to slay the dragon of Bantu education. Luthuli suffered a stroke and spent several months recovering in a Durban hospital while the ANC National Executive and ANC provincial bodies struggled to coordinate their efforts. While some ANC leaders favored a cautious approach, young ANC firebrand Joe Matthews—son of Z. K. Matthews—argued that the Bantu education system would collapse if the ANC led a comprehensive ban by African students, teachers, and administrators while establishing African-controlled alternative schools and cultural clubs.[53] Meanwhile, Verwoerd threatened boycotters at all levels with permanent bans from government schools and ordered boycotting male students over sixteen to register with the Labour Bureau as workers or face arrest. African parents were divided over the boycott. In the Transvaal particularly, women and men with sjamboks and sticks thrashed school-going children, blocked school entrances, and established "independence schools." But many parents defied the boycotts, preferring an inferior education to no education at all, as threatened by Verwoerd. And they wanted their children in schools instead of wandering in the streets unsupervised while their parents worked. Former ANC president Alfred Xuma criticized the boycott as a "negative plan" and urged protesters to work through school boards, and with teachers, as a more constructive approach. The *Bantu World* claimed to oppose Bantu education, but criticized the boycott because it involved children; it also argued that the boycott leaders were acting in defiance of ANC directives.[54] The boycott collapsed; to halt apartheid, its opponents would have to intensify their efforts.

The Congress of the People

Within the ANC, Luthuli managed an omnibus movement smoldering with tensions between color-conscious

58

Africanists assailing oppression and a plural cast of non-racialists calling for an inclusive African nationalism.[55] Despite restrictive bans, constant nighttime police raids on his house, and deteriorating health, Luthuli helped forge the Congress Alliance, an ANC-led coalition that also included the SAIC, CPC, the Federation of South African Women (FEDSAW), the South African Congress of Trade Unions (SACTU), and the white leftist Congress of Democrats (COD).[56] During his December 1954 presidential address, Luthuli remarked, "Let me here most emphatically state that while the ANC must naturally work for its own growth, yet it is equally committed to the policy of forming a multiracial united Democratic front to challenge the forces of reaction in this country."[57] In early preparations for the Congress of the People (COP), Luthuli viewed this multiracial, multi-organizational alliance as the means to "demand that we think courageously together, plan boldly together in an effort to bring freedom to all in our land."[58]

Rusty Bernstein, the primary drafter of the Freedom Charter and a leading Congress Alliance member, called Luthuli, Z. K. Matthews, Mandela, Tambo, and Sisulu the five great men who shaped the reinvigorated antiapartheid struggle. Bernstein viewed Luthuli as the disciplined, principled "father figure of them all ... who commanded a unique respect across all sectors, from the old guard to the new young militants."[59] State repression and ANC failures in Sophiatown and with Bantu education were factors in the drop in ANC membership numbers to roughly twenty-five thousand. Hoping to regain the momentum from the Defiance Campaign, the ANC convened a secret meeting in December 1954 with about forty Congress allies. So that Luthuli could attend, they met in a rural school for Indians near Stanger. Bernstein later wrote, "A meeting without Luthuli was unthinkable. Mahomet could not come to the mountain, so the mountain came to Stanger." Here, Luthuli asked Z. K. Matthews to elaborate on his earlier idea of a Congress of the People to adopt a "Freedom Charter."[60] Luthuli proclaimed that the 1910 Union, by denying democracy to Africans, had laid a "false foundation" and that the recent whites-only National Convention was "the national error." In sharp contrast, the Congress of the People would be a mass democratic convention in which all South Africans would be invited to create a Freedom Charter and an unprecedented multiracial democracy.[61]

Particularly urging Natal not to lag behind political activity in other provinces, Luthuli called for "freedom volunteers" to fan the country and gather input for the Charter, which he described as "a South African Declaration of Human Rights."[62] Dorothy Nyembe and other ANC Women's League members were particularly active, drawing as many as five thousand people to mass meetings in Cato Manor and visiting houses, where they collected demands to be included in the Freedom Charter. Nyembe introduced herself as "the voice of Chief Luthuli," prompting rapturous responses: "Ohhh! Chief Luthuli!"[63] The Congress of the People meeting at

Kliptown on June 26, 1955, was a joyous celebration of South Africa's multiracial, democratic possibilities. Albertina Sisulu remembered the opening day: "if it was the day to go to heaven, I'll just walk to heaven today."[64]

Unfortunately, a stroke and a heart attack, as well as new government orders that restricted him to Groutville, meant that Luthuli never attended the Congress of the People. When Walter Sisulu went to visit the unconscious chief, he prepared himself for the seemingly inevitable funeral.[65] But from his sickbed, the recovering Luthuli ignored state-imposed bans prohibiting him from speaking publicly with a recorded speech to the Kliptown audience in which he proclaimed the Freedom Charter a "Magna Carta—a Bill of Human Rights" that would lead to an actual South African parliament.[66] Despite his absence, Luthuli, along with Yusuf Dadoo and Trevor Huddleston, won the *Isitwalandwe* award in recognition of his leadership in the antiapartheid struggle.[67] But one audience remained unmoved: in response to Luthuli's invitation to the South African government to send delegates to the Congress of the People, three hundred police showed up to monitor the proceedings.[68]

The Freedom Charter

Influenced by the ideals enshrined in the American Declaration of Independence and the UN Declaration of Human Rights, the Freedom Charter became the concrete road map to a nonracial, democratic South Africa. The Charter demanded that all South African citizens have the right to own land; to vote and hold office; to enjoy legal equality; and to exercise full economic and educational rights, the freedoms of speech, movement, and assembly, and to have liberal democratic institutions. It also called for land redistribution through widespread individual land ownership, limited government intervention in the economy, and selective nationalization of mines and banks. It was a leftist, but not communist document; it did not call for state-controlled or collectivist land ownership, or for the abolition of private ownership or capitalist means of production. The Charter was also not a document of revolution, but of reform, speaking of "partnership, power-sharing, and the extension of freedoms" in South Africa.[69]

Luthuli felt the Freedom Charter joined the UN Declaration of Human Rights as another timeless document that provided a basis for the continuing struggle for freedom and human dignity against racial oppression.[70] He also viewed the Congress Alliance as part of a global anticolonial, anti-imperialist, anti–white supremacist coalition in the spirit of the recent Afro-Asian solidarity campaign in Bandung, Indonesia, attended by Moses Kotane and Maulvi Cachalia. Luthuli argued that the ANC was broadening its program of African nationalism to include multiracial and multi-ideological antiapartheid alliances in South Africa in the global context of Asian, African, and Caribbean decolonization and a Third World alliance of African, Asian, and Caribbean peoples.[71] He remarked, "Africa and Asia, as was seen in the Bandung Conference in April, 1955, are coming together; how could we, in the home front, discourage and belittle this spirit of cooperation between Africa and Asia? . . . As regards ideological outlook we may have different views and ideas within Congress, but at this stage our forces should be directed mainly against racial domination and apartheid."[72] ANC foreign policy flowed from the Bandung declarations, and Luthuli remarked that colonial powers around the world "are in flight or are in uneasy control as is the case with our Nationalist Government . . . sitting on an uneasy throne: their very ruthlessness is a measure of this fear and uneasiness."[73]

But the "Africanist" bloc of the ANC, including A. P. Mda, Peter Ramahonoe, and rising leaders such as Robert Sobukwe, Peter Molotsi, and Potlako Leballo, objected to the Freedom Charter's multiracial declarations ("The Land Belongs to All Who Live in It, Black and White!), claiming that it diluted African claims to South Africa based on original land occupation and their demographic majority. The Africanists further charged that the Freedom Charter's multiracialism reflected the strong influence of white communists and betrayed Lembedist African nationalism, the 1943 *African Claims* document, and the 1949 Program of Action, a criticism echoed by former ANC president Alfred Xuma. The Africanists posed a growing internal challenge to Luthuli and the Congress Alliance.[74] In Natal, Luthuli faced considerable opposition to the Freedom Charter, the Congress Alliance, and his inclusive African nation-alism. His old antagonist George Champion proclaimed the ANC, with its leaders banned, to be an "utter fail-ure," and asserted that "their influence is nil."[75] Former Luthuli ally Ngubane criticized the chief's commitment to the multiracial Congress Alliance and claimed that white leftists had inserted nationalization clauses in the Freedom Charter, thereby potentially committing the ANC to a communist principle different from the Afri-can nationalism articulated in the Program of Action.[76] Responding in the popular African publication *Drum*, Luthuli asked pointed questions of Ngubane, now a Liberal Party member: "Shall we infer from this allega-tion of his that in the Liberal Party he is suspicious of his fellow-members who belong to other racial groups than his own: white, coloured and Indian? If he is not, why should he insinuate that relations among the allied Congresses are governed by suspicion of one another?" Luthuli asserted that the ANC headed "an omnibus liberatory movement" that included members "with different political inclinations, but all subjecting their personal inclinations to the overriding needs of our day which are to fight and defeat apartheid." He noted that there had long been communist ANC leaders like Moses Kotane and that two CPSA members had been signatories to *African Claims*, touted by the disgruntled Xuma as the "true" African voice: "I do not see anything red there . . . or are we seeing with different spectacles?" Declaring himself a socialist in the mold of European social democratic states, Luthuli reaffirmed his view that the Freedom Charter had socialist clauses in it, but denied that it reflected a "Moscow communistic outlook."[77] In an editorial in the antiapartheid newspaper *Liberation*, Luthuli skewered critics of the Congress Alliance: "People seem to be alarmed at the fact that there may be a so-called Right wing, Centre and Left wing in the Congress. To me it is a healthy sign in any organization when people freely express their point of view."[78]

Luthuli was not a communist, but he was not overtly hostile to the Soviet Union or to communists. When South Africa closed the Soviet consulate, claiming that it fomented subversive activities among South African blacks, Luthuli protested this "malicious propaganda against a friendly nation," urged South Africa to reverse its decision in the interests of world peace, and called on all peoples worldwide to be in solidarity with "all freedom and peace-loving people in the world such as the people of the U.S.S.R."[79] Friendly with the communist SAIC president Dr. Yusuf Dadoo, Luthuli spoke of the Congress Alliance as "our liberation army" preventing "submission of the masses" to the "baaskap . . . Nationalist party."[80] But Luthuli's public defense of the Freedom Charter and the Congress Alliance masked private concerns about the centralization of power in the Transvaal, the closer nexus between the Transvaal-based ANC, and communists in ANC leadership, the COD, and the underground SACP, as well as some economic clauses in the Charter and possible implications for the balance of power within the Congress Alliance. He affirmed the principles of the Charter, but asked that all ANC members have an opportunity to review the Charter section by section to "appreciate the socialist basis of the Charter before they say yes or no." Like Matthews, Luthuli objected to the nationalization clauses in the Freedom Charter, and was "disturbed very much about certain trends or cliques in our Congress. Some people are taking advantage of the fact that I cannot move about to exert my influence; they are using this period to make the ANC a leftist organization under the domination of the Ex Communist Party." Threatening to resign if there was no satisfactory resolution, Luthuli wondered why the ANC would agree to "making the Freedom Charter the basis for cooperation with any group in the future. Why should we tie ourselves so fast to the Congress of Democrats? We should form a Freedom front as wide as possible."[81]

But he did not object when the ANC ratified the Freedom Charter by an overwhelming majority at a special conference in March 1956. For Luthuli, the Charter was the glue of the ANC-led Congress Alliance, representative of an inclusive African nationalism that would facilitate the goal of African majority rule. For him, multiracialism was "purely a matter of present policy, representing as we do, a large section of people who think tribally. We have to carry our people with us."[82] He viewed a broad, democratic Congress Alliance as a matter of principle, but also understood the need for resources, money, and strategic experience. He also saw distinct roles for each organization within the Congress Alliance. He felt that COD members should organize and propagandize in white areas about the evils of the pass laws. Coloured organizations should mobilize Coloureds against the Population Registration Act and the Group Areas Act. The task of the Indian Congress was to raise awareness about the danger of the Population Registration Act.[83]

Multiracial Local and Transnational Alliances

The government's bans prevented the chief from visiting South African cities. With ANC lieutenants Conco and Yengwa also banned, this increased the isolation of the Natal ANC from the Transvaal-based ANC national executive. Scrambling to retain links to the outside world, Luthuli relied even more on Indian friends, such as the bookkeeper E. V. Mohamed, a Natal Indian Congress member, unofficial secretary of the Stanger ANC branch, and Luthuli's personal accountant; and the shopkeeper Goolam Suleiman, the unofficial treasurer of the Stanger ANC branch. Since the police did not monitor Indians with the same intensity as Africans, Luthuli conducted Congress business and held secret meetings in the homes of Mohamed and Suleiman, enjoying tea and Indian dishes during lunches filled with political discussion about domestic and international affairs.[84] Mohamed and Suleiman also acted as couriers and transporters, facilitating the flow of sensitive correspondence and surreptitious visitors, as well as the organization of secret ANC NEC meetings in the homes of other Indians. Thanks to their acquaintance with an Indian Special Branch officer unaware of their close connection to the leadership, who unwittingly informed them of police activities regarding Luthuli, they helped the chief defy his bans despite increasingly intrusive surveillance and phone tapping by the Special Branch.[85]

Nokukhanya Luthuli, by being the family's primary breadwinner and caregiver, made it possible for Albert to be ANC president—a prestigious but unpaid position. She also managed to be an ANC Women's League leader and ANC national conference delegate who participated in women's pass campaigns and mediated political disputes with influential associates such as Ngubane.[86] The inclusion of Nokukhanya and other African women had made the ANC a mass organization, and Luthuli encouraged the female-led campaigns against the 1952 Abolition of Documents and Passes Act, which extended pass laws to women. Chiding those men who criticized female involvement in politics but remained absent from the political arena themselves, Luthuli hoped that the antipass campaign would encourage close cooperation between the ANC Women's League, FEDSAW, and the local African Women's Association (AWA).[87] Despite Luthuli's cooperative stance, Women's League leaders including G. Kuzwayo and B. Mkhize defected to organize antipass campaigns for the AWA.[88] The AWA and the Bantu Women's League charged that Luthuli was on the payroll of Indians and that the ANC were communist stooges who had deviated from the African nationalism articulated in the Program of Action.[89] Yet Luthuli's support was unwavering: "Clearly the women are in the front rank of the battle now opening. They are the victims the government has singled out for its latest attack. But the struggle is not one for women alone … this must be a joint campaign of men and women, whose aim is to end the pass system and the Government which upholds it."[90] ANC leader Dorothy Nyembe recalled, "I was a full time member and not just a tea-maker. Our mentor was Chief Albert Luthuli. He taught us that men and women were equal, and that it all depends on one's dedication."[91]

By 1954, anticommunist American government repression had forced the pioneering anticolonial/antiapartheid Council on African Affairs (CAA) to disband, and the antiapartheid work of the National Association for the Advancement of Colored People (NAACP) lessened as it focused more on the burgeoning domestic civil rights movement. Inspired by the nonviolent civil disobedience ethos of the Defiance Campaign, the white American pacifist George Houser, who had provided financial and moral support, subsequently headed the American Committee on Africa (ACOA). The ACOA advocated the nonviolent end of colonialism in Africa and apartheid in South Africa, and its anticommunism allowed it to succeed the CAA as the leading American antiapartheid organization. In 1954, Houser visited South Africa to observe apartheid firsthand and to make direct contact with antiapartheid leaders, including

Luthuli, who impressed him as a man of deep integrity.[92] In 1955, the white American Quaker Mary-Louise Hooper, an activist with the NAACP and the American Friends Service Committee (AFSC), visited South Africa and was also deeply impressed by Luthuli and the ANC. Committed to fighting injustice anywhere—"the Freedom Struggle is one-Mississippi, South Africa"— the independently wealthy Hooper promptly bought a house in Durban to become a "fairy godmother" to the ANC, providing financial support, transportation in her "Congress Special" sedan, and her own time as Luthuli's personal secretary. Though the Luthulis earned money from Nokukhanya's farming, from running a nearby store, and from their cane fields, Hooper provided needed financial assistance, particularly to pay the children's school fees. She became a trusted friend of the Luthulis and of other Natal ANC leaders, including M. B. Yengwa and Conco, along with ANC and trade union leaders Stephen Dlamini and Archie Gumede. She was part of an interracial political partnership that included the NIC leaders G. M. Naicker, Ismail and Fatima Meer, and J. N. Singh; E. V. Mohamed; and white liberals Hilda and Leo Kuper, Violane Junod, and Alan Paton, who worked and played together, including boisterous parties filled with Zulu singing and dancing.[93]

The Luthuli ANC and its allies were filled with deeply dedicated people who organized their struggle at great personal expense, despite political bans, logistical difficulties, restrictions on their movements, and the constant threat of imprisonment or death. They did so while keeping regular jobs, providing for their families, and dealing with all of life's vicissitudes. It is extraordinary that the Congress movement was able to grow in such an environment. Hooper also helped Luthuli break his bans and evade the police in her speedy "Congress Special" so that Luthuli could attend all-night Congress meetings at safe houses over weekends and attendees could be back at their jobs on Monday.[94] With considerable difficulty, executive members came to two or three of these all-day and all-night meetings each year to read reports, make critical decisions, and plan campaigns.[95] The ANC leadership also held secret meetings at Hooper's house, particularly during holidays, when there were fewer police officers on duty and it was easier to disguise a political meeting as a social gathering. On Christmas Day, 1956, Luthuli called such a meeting at Hooper's house, but his family was unimpressed by his political dedication: he returned to his home after midnight to find his family in bed and a cold turkey on the kitchen table.[96] Luthuli's daughter Albertina confirmed that "the police never caught him breaking his banning order, though he broke it all the time. We saw the police lurking around our house and we hated them, but UBaba always kept his cool and confronted them with dignity."[97] In 1957, after the government arrested Hooper for her ANC work, she successfully sued the state for unlawful detention, winning an award of 1,700 pounds, which she donated to a very appreciative ANC.

Enraged government officials then deported Hooper, banning her permanently from the country, but she became an official ANC representative and fundraiser in America and at the All-African conferences in Accra in 1958, Tunis in 1960, and Cairo in 1961.[98]

Hooper was an ACOA intermediary with Luthuli in the ANC's attempts to secure funding for an ANC newspaper.[99] When Houser suggested that the staunchly anticommunist ACOA might have difficulty fundraising for a communist-linked ANC, Luthuli admitted, "I do not like Communists," but, acting on principle, refused to dismiss white communist/leftist lawyers such as Rowley Arenstein, Joe Slovo, and Vernon Berrange as a precondition for ACOA assistance. He asserted that the ANC, not white communists, led the Congress Alliance. He felt that to distance themselves from dedicated supporters solely because they were communists would undermine the credibility and integrity of the ANC, which prioritized professional ability and personal commitment to the struggle over communist affiliation. He told Hooper, "my policy is that we must make friends from both the West and East and take from each what is good for us so long as we are not called upon to violate the principles on which we are prosecuting our Freedom Struggle."[100]

The Treason Trial and the Strengthened Congress Alliance

The government interpreted the Freedom Charter as a subversive document. On December 5, 1956, police

TREASON TRIAL

The ACCUSED

DECEMBER 1956

The original 156 defendants in the South African Treason Trial (1956–61). (Getty)

arrested Luthuli and 155 antiapartheid leaders, charging them with high treason. At 4 a.m., heavily armed police, announcing in Zulu, "This is the day!," invaded and ransacked Luthuli's home and searched for incriminating materials. Guards in Johannesburg Prison stripped the incarcerated male activists in an attempt to humiliate them. The Natal ANC and the Indian Congress immediately petitioned for their release, saying, "these arrests . . . follow the familiar fascist pattern set by Hitlerite Germany."[101] Luthuli's first time in prison lasted for a year, and he saw Nokukhanya just twice during that time.[102] Despite the prospect of going to the gallows, Luthuli expressed no concern, but worried more about his family's welfare and insisted that the state had a weak case.[103] In holding suspects during the five-year Treason Trial (1956–61), as it came to be known, the prison brought far-flung activists together. As he had after the stripping of his chieftainship four years earlier, Luthuli responded to great adversity with a measured and inspirational statesmanship that his political colleagues deeply admired. Before Mandela's more famous prison leadership on Robben Island after 1964, Luthuli—with Z. K. Matthews, Moses Kotane, and G. M. Naicker—maintained discipline among imprisoned Congress Alliance members and initiated political discussions, concerts, religious services, and cultural theater to foster political fellowship. M. B. Yengwa remembered that Luthuli was "notable for rising to occasions. He has a tremendous reserve of power and ability. . . . You find when a crisis arises he is able to tide it over with far more strength than you thought he had."[104] When Yengwa uncorked praises (*izibongo*) honoring Shaka, Luthuli rejoiced in the performance with Zulu and non-Zulu prisoners, declaring, "Ngu Shaka lowo!" (That is Shaka!). In a moment of incipient nationalism far removed from any tribalism, the prisoners felt "bound together by love of our history."[105]

Luthuli developed deeper trust with communist members, particularly Kotane, whose counsel Luthuli sought before he made any major decision. ANC secretary-general Sisulu later remarked that Luthuli always asked, "Does Moses Kotane know about this? He was never happy till he knows that he knows. Chief Luthuli gained confidence in the communist leadership in that trial because he came into contact with Bram, Rusty, Joe and thought, well, these people mean well."[106] Luthuli began to read Marxist and SACP literature to better understand communism and his communist allies, and he relied on communists for logistical support to break his bans and attend secret ANC and Congress Alliance meetings.[107] Communists, too, looked upon Luthuli with greater admiration and understanding. The Johannesburg-based communist Ben Turok remarked that Luthuli had a "gravitas and naturally royal bearing combined with a simplicity that was endearing."[108] Personal relations aside, there were good political reasons for Luthuli's support of the Congress Alliance. The support of African communists including Kotane, J. B. Marks, David Bopape, and Sisulu, a Communist Party member since at least 1955, had been crucial to Luthuli's large majority during the 1952 presidential elections.[109] Along with the ANC Youth Leaguers, the resurgent SACP had radicalized the political struggle in the 1940s. After the government banning of the SACP in 1950, COD communists remained a source of both critical resources and radical energy, contributing to the ideas of multiracialism and, later, armed self-defense in the Congress Alliance. Luthuli was clear: "For myself I am not a Communist," but "I have one enemy, the Nationalist government, and I will not fight on two fronts. I shall work with all who are prepared to stand with me in the struggle for the liberation of our country. We leave our differing political theories to one side until the day of liberation."[110] The Treason Trial also increased international attention and support, particularly through the Treason Trial Defense Fund, started by antiapartheid cleric Bishop Ambrose Reeves, part of ongoing support from English clergy such as Canon John Collins and Trevor Huddleston.[111]

During the trial, Luthuli professed his and the ANC's principled commitment to nonviolence, though not everyone within the organization shared this commitment; Mandela, for instance, regarded nonviolence as a tactical strategy.[112] To persistent questions about the prospect of "violence and bloodshed," Luthuli declared, "the ANC would carry on its struggle on a non-violent basis, even in the face of a clash." The government was also perturbed by Luthuli's growing stature, reflected in ANC Women's League leader Lillian Ngoyi's insistence that ANC political meetings should open not with "God Save the King" but "God Save Luthuli" because "Luthuli is our Jesus."[113] But Luthuli, Tambo, and fifty-nine others were acquitted in December 1957 after the pre-trial examination, an inexplicable outcome that actually disturbed Luthuli, for whom "the truth is I would be happier to see the whole thing through with my comrades."[114] By 1959, there were only thirty defendants left, but they faced a more serious allegation: instead of the original charge of intending violence against the state, the prosecution now alleged that violence was the policy of the ANC and its allies. Finally, in 1961, the court acquitted all Treason Trial defendants, declaring that the state had not proven its allegation.

Luthuli celebrates the wedding of his daughter, 1958. (Bailey's African History Archives, photograph by Drum Photographer)

Mandela before Mandela: Luthuli and the Statesmanship of Racial Reconciliation

While Luthuli was in prison, Ghana won independence a year after Sudan became the first sub-Saharan African country to gain independence. Most of Africa, with the glaring regional exception of southern Africa, became decolonized by the mid-1960s. Luthuli connected the South African struggle to larger African and Asian de-colonization movements, partially to motivate black South Africans: "We point out these events taking place in Africa to show our complacent people here that the rest of Africa is astir."[115] Luthuli wrote directly to South African prime minister Johannes Strydom imploring him to scrap apartheid, a system belonging to the "dark ages." Bypassing the Native Affairs Department, which supposedly handled all African matters, Luthuli told Strydom that "ALL SOUTH AFRICAN POLITICS ARE NATIVE AFFAIRS," urged him to rethink the government's "Native Policy" as "NATIONAL POLICY," and called for a "multiracial convention to seek a solution to our pressing national problems."[116] Strydom ignored Luthuli's letter; not until the secret talks with Mandela in the mid-1980s would the government communicate directly with an ANC leader. Released in December 1957, Luthuli did not rest. His ANC presidential address that month insisted that he did not hate whites, only the white supremacist systems of racial domination and exploitation that created a police state, a virtual prison for

78

Africans subject to a "slave education." In parallel with another Christian activist, Martin Luther King Jr., Luthuli explained that his agapic love for humankind and proactive nonviolent strategies informed his vision of a democratic, egalitarian, nonracial South Africa. Like King, who formed the Southern Christian Leadership Conference (SCLC) as a vehicle for Christians to fight for racial justice, in December 1957 Luthuli became a leader in the Interdenominational African Ministers' Federation (IDAMF) to undertake similar work against apartheid.[117] He exhorted his followers to break their shackles since "the length of slavery depends largely on the oppressed themselves and not on the oppressor. . . . WE HAVE THE KEY TO FREEDOM—not the oppressor. It all depends on how much we sacrifice ourselves for Freedom."[118] In advance of the first all-white national ballot in April 1958, taking advantage of expired bans, he barnstormed cities, appealing to the conscience of voters. He urged South African citizens to see apartheid legislation as "the most tyrannical slave laws ever to besmirch the statute book of our country."[119] Most whites remained unmoved by his entreaties, as the electorate handed the National Party another victory; for the first time, it won more than 50 percent of the white vote.

As Luthuli listened empathetically to the endless stories of rural, poverty-stricken Africans abused by white landowners and subjected to forced labor after convictions for pass-law violations, his intimate understanding of the destructive impact of apartheid policies fueled his nationwide tours in 1958 and 1959.[120] He roused multi-racial crowds in South African cities, becoming the only person in South Africa capable of attracting broad support from Africans, Indians, Coloureds, and an increasing number of whites, particularly in the COD, the Black Sash, antiapartheid white women who wore a black sash on their dresses to mourn apartheid, and in the Liberal Party, entranced by his "gospel of democracy and freedom." For perhaps the first time in South African history, a significant number of whites came to hear an African politician. Long before Nelson Mandela would be celebrated for assuaging white fears of vengeful black domination and subsequent loss of power and identity—the guilty nightmare that drove many into apartheid's arrogant utopia of endless white rule—Luthuli lessened white fear and mistrust of Africans, "magically . . . inspiring confidence and trust," at least in some whites.[121] The chief "had a regal stature complementing a strong personality. He was the type of man that commanded one's attention; when he spoke, people listened."[122] In Johannesburg, he was treated like a distinguished foreign guest when he invited his privileged audience to climb with him up a mountain of which "Freedom Is the Apex." At the apex were the ideals of the Freedom Charter and the vision of a democratic, nonracial South Africa that would be a global model for multiracial harmony and coexistence.[123] This inspirational challenge to climb together contrasted sharply with the dystopian vision of new prime minister

Hendrik Verwoerd, for whom multiracial contact was an inherently dangerous encounter with evil, supposedly remedied by the utopian purity of his apartheid policies. Luthuli lamented that Verwoerd and the NP were blind to "the wealth that lies in our very diversity, nor the underlying humanity and South Africanism that binds us all. . . . Their profession . . . is the spreading of the spirit of Afrikaner exclusiveness . . . and when they try to don the mantle of statesmen, they succeed only in making themselves ridiculous, like pigmies strutting in giants' robes."[124]

In Cape Town, Luthuli particularly found solace in the thousands of compatriots who welcomed his speeches with roars of "Mayibuye Afrika!" (Come back Africa!) and "Somlandela Luthuli!" (We will follow

Multiracial mass meeting, Cape Town, 1959. Crowds came to hear Luthuli, chanting "Somlandela Luthuli!" (We will follow Luthuli wherever he goes!). (Bailey's African History Archives, photograph by Cloete Breytenbach)

Luthuli wherever he goes!).[125] Luthuli visited Parliament while it debated the controversial University Apartheid Bill, creating a buzz of interest among Nationalist senators seeing the square, dignified, lonely figure of a Black man sitting amongst them. In the Native Representatives' rooms, there were brief introductions to members of Parliament. He met with Nationalists and, against the wishes of Prime Minister Verwoerd, with members of the South African Bureau of Racial Affairs (SABRA), the proapartheid Afrikaner think tank. Yet legislators passed the University Apartheid Bill. When Luthuli assented to the request of the Black Sash to inspect their ranks as they kept vigil outside Parliament, an unnamed "Afrikaner from the Free State" rushed to the chief and "apologized for what was being done by White men in the House." But sadly, neither the chief's stirring presence nor this unexpected breaking of the ranks was enough to halt the accelerating apartheid onslaught.[126]

Many whites, of course, were not nearly ready for Luthuli's reconciliatory message. F. W. De Klerk, destined to be South Africa's last apartheid leader, was a college student when he heard Luthuli, but "his message that all South Africans should have the right to one-man one-vote in an undivided South Africa was at the time utterly alien to us."[127] In Johannesburg, Luthuli confronted "Nazi-like [white] thugs" shouting, "We will not allow a kaffir to address this meeting!" The dissidents stormed his platform and pummeled the sixty-one-year old Luthuli to the ground, leaving him with a bloodied face, a swollen jaw, and an "egg-sized bump on his forehead." To the great relief of his followers, Luthuli promptly dusted himself off, insisted on calm, suggested gently that his attackers had not "matured spiritually yet," and delivered a vigorous one-hour speech—using the incident to emphasize the urgent need for South African racial reconciliation and to emphasize African demands for equality. His amazed audience showered him with a standing ovation.[128] As Luthuli received rapturous acclaim for speeches in the transitional building site that came to be known as Durban's "Red Square," parliamentarians demanded that the government "do something about this Luthuli . . . because his speeches were setting the minds of the people on fire."[129] Unable to meet with government officials, Luthuli had successfully taken his case directly to the people, "an incorruptible, fearless and altogether unfrightening Crusader" for a revolutionary vision of his beloved country.[130]

Effective May 30, 1959, just before Luthuli's address to thirty thousand people at an ANC antipass rally in Sophiatown protesting white South Africa's celebration of Union Day, the government issued a five-year ban, claiming ironically that Luthuli's racial reconciliation tour was "promoting hostility between whites and non-whites." The ban placed Luthuli under virtual house arrest in Groutville and forbade meetings, claiming the "objects of Communism would be furthered if ex-Chief Luthuli addressed any meetings in the Union."[131] The ANC declared the bans a "shameful act of political persecution" and called for mass protests.[132] Luthuli vowed to risk jail to defy his bans and predicted that "in the end White South Africa will realize we must come together and discuss our problems."[133] Supporters sang "Somlandela Luthuli," and carloads of them traveled with him to Groutville. The liberal white press argued against the ban on Luthuli, "an African leader of unusual caliber" and a "pillar of reasonableness," predicting that the government's action would be "one of its most tragic mistakes."[134] Alan Paton's Liberal Party condemned the ban as "senseless, unjust and an act of inhumanity amounting . . . to five years' confinement without trial."[135] The journal *Liberation* extolled Luthuli as "a militant and uncompromising fighter for freedom . . . a truly South African leader, speaking for and seeking the wellbeing of all in this gloriously diverse South Africa of ours."[136]

Confined to Groutville, Luthuli penned an inspirational letter to an ANCYL conference, quoting Abraham Lincoln's Gettysburg Address—"government of the people, by the people and for the people shall not perish from the earth"—and demanding that Africans fight for this same freedom in South Africa.[137] On Freedom Day, June 26, 1959, he called for a boycott of potatoes, which lasted over three months, and protested against the pass laws, which led to the arrest of five hundred thousand Africans annually, many of whom were sent to "farm jails" and manufacturing sites, where their continuous, coerced, unpaid labor produced South African agricultural exports, cigarettes, and other goods sold domestically and overseas.[138] The governor-general, C. R. Swart, officially opened farm jails, claiming proudly that they lessened state expenditures to house Africans, provided much-needed labor to white farmers, and rehabilitated "criminals."[139] In reality, captive Africans dug potatoes with their fingers and "boss-boys" whipped, assaulted, and even murdered them with impunity.

Luthuli also engaged the international arena. In 1958, he had called for a global boycott of all South African goods, a move strengthened by a motion at the 1959 Accra conference that helped to establish the antiapartheid movement in several countries, including Ireland, Great Britain, Scandinavia, the Netherlands, India, the United States, and Ghana.[140] Luthuli viewed economic sanctions and boycotts against South Africa as a form of international nonviolence that could force South Africa to renounce apartheid and thus avoid protracted violence and possible civil war.[141] He understood that "the economic boycott of South Africa will entail undoubted hardship for Africans. We do not doubt that. But if it is a method which shortens the day of blood, the suffering to us will be a price we are willing to pay. In any case, we suffer already, our children are often undernourished, and on a small scale (so far) we die at the whim of a policeman." He later argued that "already in any case, they [the poor] are in difficulties; at some time this vicious circle must be cut; at some time some generation must suffer to do that. . . . If you suggested that the African people should not suffer you in fact are saying that they should remain slaves. . . . So with this question of 'It will hit the Africans hardest,' let us be hit, let some of us die, even if necessary die through bullets, if necessary die through starvation, if this will end this vicious circle."[142]

Inspired by the appeal of Luthuli and SACTU for economic sanctions, the British boycott movement coordinated closely with the South African domestic struggle and with the exiled ANC, broadening the terrain for sanctions beyond economics to other sectors, such as sport, culture, and academics.[143] In Ireland, Kader Asmal—who had earlier been inspired by the chief to join the ANC's Defiance Campaign and was now a law lecturer at Trinity College—promptly founded the Irish antiapartheid movement.[144] Black South Africans were delighted to learn that the Seamen's Union of Australia and Waterside Workers' Federation embargoed South African ships.[145] In the United States, the ACOA, citing Luthuli's endorsement of economic sanctions as the means to force the end of apartheid, called for an American consumer boycott of South African goods and for U.S. government economic sanctions against South Africa.[146] Luthuli again aligned the South African freedom struggle with UN-led human rights efforts, calling on all South Africans to observe Human Rights Day on December 10, 1959.[147] On the eve of the fiftieth anniversary of the Union of South Africa in 1960, he lamented that politically disenfranchised Africans were doomed to perpetual subordination under "Nationalist Party rule," but also predicted, rightly, that within another fifty years South Africa would have a "free non-racial democracy."[148]

The Africanist Revolt and the Founding of the PAC

Despite continued Africanist complaints about the perceived negative impact of white communists, the Freedom Charter and the multiracial alliance generally on African nationalism and the Program of Action, Luthuli had expressed little concern over this dissident faction within the ANC: "I don't regard the Africanists as a serious problem within the ANC. They do exist, but not as a challenger meriting constant attention. . . . The ANC should strongly pursue its policy of cooperation with other racial groups, and win the African people to that point of view. That is the only sound policy."[149] On November 1, 1958, Luthuli addressed the ANC Transvaal Provincial Conference in Orlando, outside Johannesburg, where he affirmed his view that the multiracial Congress Alliance was the most effective means to end apartheid and, as a model for the post-apartheid state, the strongest guarantor of a sustainable democratic, inclusive, nonracial South Africa. But about fifty Africanists entered the hall while Luthuli spoke, and, as Luthuli supporters affirmed "Africa is for all," heckled them with rejoinders that "Africa is for the Africans and the white man must go back to Europe." Longstanding internal tensions were about to boil over. The next morning, before elections for key National Executive positions, over a hundred ANC volunteers with sticks and pieces of iron guarded the door as a similar number of Africanists clustered outside. The Africanists remained frustrated in their ambition to win a majority of NEC posts and continued to claim that the Freedom Charter deviated from *African Claims* and the Program of Action. They also objected to the term "multiracialism," which they felt legitimized apartheid's obsession with supposed racial difference and diluted the primary claim of Africans to rule the country.

Ultimately, the ANC NEC expelled Josias Madzunya and Potlako Leballo from the ANC for their loud objections to the Congress Alliance.[150] On November 8, 1958, the Africanists confirmed their secession from the ANC, establishing the Pan-African Congress (PAC) on April 6, 1959, under the presidency of Robert Sobukwe. ANC leaders reiterated that from its 1912 founding the ANC had cooperated with other racial groups, and they argued that *African Claims* did not reject cooperation with other racial groups. They affirmed that the "COD is a creation of the ANC and the Indian Congress" and that the Africanist version of African nationalism was "nothing more than Dr. Verwoerd's policy of Development along their own lines."[151] Luthuli later lamented the Africanist position: "Those who say 'Africa for the Africans' are not realistic. Where would the Whites of South Africa go? This is also their home. It is of no use to argue that they shouldn't have come. They are here and that is an inescapable fact."[152]

But Pan-Africanism was sweeping across the continent, emboldening the Africanists within the ANC. The ANC annual conference happened concurrently with the All-African Peoples Conference (AAPC) in newly independent Ghana. For Nkrumah, the conference was to create a Pan-African movement of Gandhian nonviolent tactics, mass mobilization, economic sanctions, and diplomatic isolation against colonialism and imperialism that could lead to a unified continental government and African democratic socialism. The AAPC targeted 1963 as the date for African liberation, inspiring the popular South African call to be "free by '63."[153] The AAPC inspired Patrice Lumumba to return to the Democratic Republic of Congo (DRC) with a powerful Pan-African vision for Congolese independence. The Africanists adopted the AAPC's Pan-Africanist vision, with its stronger emphasis on African nationalism, and cast further aspersions on the ANC's multiracial alliance. The presence of Mary-Louise Hooper as an official ANC delegate in Accra may have lent further credence to the notion that whites had undue influence in the ANC.

The ANC had long been attuned to the Pan-African currents emanating from Ghana, the Black Star of Africa. The first Pan-African conference on African soil, the 1958 Conference of Independent States in Ghana, established April 15 as African Freedom Day to mark the progress of African independence movements and the determination of anticolonial movements

89

to achieve freedom—and Luthuli had long framed the South African liberation struggle within larger African independence movements and continental Pan-Africanism.[154] However, ANC leaders disagreed with the AAPC's proclamation of an "African Personality based on the philosophy of Pan-African socialism" as a guiding ideal of African decolonization and independence. The ANC leadership asserted that the presence of South Africa's large white population—by far the largest on the continent—necessitated a broader African nationalism that included non-Africans in the fight to create a multiracial society. In his writings, and in his direct communications with future Tanzanian president Julius Nyerere, Luthuli contextualized South Africa within other multiracial societies in East and Central Africa. ANC leaders argued as well that this "African personality" and "Pan-African socialism" also excluded Asians, and that the AAPC should adopt instead the broader Afro-Asian anticolonial front called for at the 1955 Bandung conference.[155] Despite this disagreement, Luthuli remained optimistic that South Africa would also be free.[156] Yet Africanists by now concluded that the ANC would not be the vessel for emancipation and instead formed the PAC to realize their freedom dreams. In the midst of his successful 1959 tour affirming the growing multiracial alliance, Luthuli lamented "continuous harping on race by the government has caused some nonwhites to emulate them and preach exclusive control of South Africa by one racial group (Africans).

We have seen developing a tremendous narrow African nationalism which is reviving tribalism. But whatever apartheid might do to disturb racial peace in South Africa, the ANC will never pursue the same disastrous policy of narrow nationalism."[157]

4

Apartheid Violence and
Armed Self-Defense

"A Slow-Moving Sharpeville:"
African Resistance to Grand Apartheid

The Sharpeville massacre in March 1960 is popularly viewed as the turning point to taking up arms in self-defense, but African resistance to the systemic "grand apartheid" provides a more accurate immediate context. In 1958, new prime minister Verwoerd unveiled grand apartheid as a political device to maintain white supremacy and Afrikaner ethnic identity and security. Grand apartheid was Verwoerd's ambitious answer to African decolonization sweeping across Africa north of the Zambezi River. Distinct from earlier petty apartheid laws, which defined and separated racial groups, the linchpin of grand apartheid was the 1958 Promotion of Bantu Self-Government Act, which created ten ethnic-based "homelands" or Bantustans that would eventually become "independent." With no parliamentary oversight, the Minister of Bantu Administration and Development ruled unilaterally over the Bantustans as his personal fiefdom, populated by Africans who were his virtual property whether their working lives were spent in the Bantustans or in "white" South Africa. The minister also had the power to ban the ANC and deny entrance to the homelands. By locating African citizenship within ethnic-based homelands, grand apartheid policies denied the ANC's inclusive nationalism, refused African claims to South African political citizenship, and cast them as foreign migrant workers under perpetual threat of being "endorsed" to underdeveloped and often unfamiliar rural areas. Verwoerd sold grand apartheid as an instrument of peace. "Must Bantu and European in future develop as intermixed communities, or as communities separated from one another in so far as this is practically possible? If the reply is 'intermingled communities,' then the following must be understood. There will be competition and conflict everywhere."[1] Despite describing apartheid to foreign audiences as a "policy of good neighborliness," Verwoerd explicitly rejected Luthuli's call for multiracial partnership. "This is our country. If we had partnership with the black man, pretty soon he would feel that it is his country."[2]

Despite the increasing white electoral support for the National Party and Verwoerd's audacious vision, grand apartheid was doomed from the start. The Bantustans, sitting on the 13 percent of land designated to Africans in the 1913 and 1936 Land Acts, became even more overcrowded, lacked an industrial base or developed infrastructure, and remained financially dependent on South Africa. They became little more than sites of circular African migration, on the one hand reservoirs of cheap labor for the "white" cities and, on the other, dumping grounds for "redundant" unemployed Africans in cities or on white-owned farms. Men often returned from the gold mines coughing up blood, a grim precursor of imminent death. The state further undermined women's fragile economic standing with new pass laws and beer-brewing prohibitions. The state drastically limited available land, then, citing land shortages, ordered Africans to reduce their cattle herds by either killing or selling them immediately, thus forcing many to sell to rival Afrikaner farmers at steeply discounted prices. Luthuli bitterly remarked, "to the day of death, whether in cities or farms or Reserves, we are tenants on the white man's land. That is our share of South Africa. Our home is the white man's garbage can."[3]

Luthuli had already noted that the government's own Tomlinson Commission (1956) had admitted that there was woefully inadequate available land for Africans, and he mocked the government's refusal to provide adequate funding for the ambitious plans of the "great fraud apartheid. Why should the Government run away from nursing its baby, apartheid, properly?"[4] Luthuli, the former government chief deposed for his insistence that his primary chiefly loyalties were to the people, not the state, blasted the new Bantu Authorities system, which invested government chiefs with dictatorial powers over their people, as the "worst caricature imaginable of our traditional form of government," one that would reduce Africans to "fourth-class citizenship." Bantu Authorities used chiefs as instruments to destroy antiapartheid opposition and administrative puppets carrying out apartheid policies that would consign Africans to a primitive, isolated, and subordinated tribalism. To government claims that Bantu Authorities would develop Africans on their own lines, Luthuli parried, "I do not know of any people who really have 'developed along their own lines.' . . . In practice it turns out not to be development along your own lines at all, but development along the lines designed by the Government through the Native Affairs Department."[5]

Despite being stripped of firearms by the colonial state after resistance in the late nineteenth century, some rural Africans now battled against grand apartheid. Pedi and Mpondo rebels killed collaborators, including chiefs, and burned the houses of others, briefly claiming control of land in these areas. Only massive joint police-military operations were able to crush the resistance. In Natal, most spectacularly in the Cato Manor area of Durban, women protested pass laws, municipal beer halls, and police raids on their own beer-brewing operations. They destroyed public buildings and dipping tanks and burned sugarcane farms and wattle plantations. Echoing a popular rallying cry during women's antipass campaigns, Luthuli proclaimed, "When you touch the women, you touch a rock."[6] In the Bahurutshe Reserve in Zeerust, African women burned their passes and assaulted government collaborators. Both Mpondo and Sekhukune rebels asked repeatedly for the ANC to provide them with arms to defend themselves against South African military and police aggression, and though the ANC instead donated one hundred pounds, these areas later became rich recruiting grounds for the ANC's post-1961 armed wing, Umkhonto we Sizwe (MK).[7] Justice "Gizenga" Mpanza, from Groutville, was one of many engaged in massive sugarcane burning in solidarity with the Mpondoland revolt. Amidst mass trials and hangings of resisters, Sisulu and Luthuli called for calm, but the ANC executive struggled to keep pace with these rural, local popular struggles, and to provide viable direction to township residents who looked for a more militant response to apartheid.[8]

As the punishing decade of the 1950s ended, Luthuli continued to argue for more exacting nonviolent strategies like another Defiance Campaign and more protest demonstrations—but warned against "any reckless haste and impatience" that would provide a pretext for deadly government force.[9] During its annual conference in December 1959, the ANC announced a massive antipass campaign scheduled for April 1960. Luthuli praised British prime minister Harold Macmillan's "Winds of Change" speech delivered in February 1960 in South Africa's parliament, in which Macmillan rejected racial discrimination, supported the idea of free nonracial communities, and acknowledged the inevitability of African independence, in line with ANC sentiment but in stark contrast to South Africa's grand apartheid plans. While Luthuli made clear that he and the ANC were not naive enough to expect the prime minister's speech to have a lasting impact, he thought it would "make white South Africa think." Little did they know that unforeseen, explosive events would soon lead to the banning of the ANC and a decisive new turn in the fight for freedom.[10]

The Sharpeville Moment

In March 1960, when police using machine guns and high-caliber rifles killed 69 unarmed African pass protesters and wounded another 186 people at a PAC rally in Sharpeville, and also fired into a crowd of 10,000 pass protesters in the Cape Town townships of Langa and Nyanga, killing 2 and wounding over 50, headlines captured worldwide outrage.[11] The bloodbath brought pariah status and martial law to South Africa, which was already bucking Macmillan's "Winds of Change" speech. The declaration of a state of emergency gave the government sweeping powers to detain over twenty-five thousand people and outlaw the ANC and the PAC, sentencing its President Robert Sobukwe to prison. Verwoerd commended the Sharpeville commander, Lieutenant Colonel Pienaar, who exonerated his officers for teaching a violent lesson to "the native mentality [, which] does not allow them to gather for a peaceful demonstration."[12] Justice Minister François Erasmus, in his previous post as defense minister, had railed against

Africans who aimed to "bring to its knees any White Government in South Africa which stands for White supremacy." He wanted the South African Defense Force to model itself on the French colonial army waging war in Algeria. He was confident that soldiers, reinforced by white civilian posses, would "shoot down the black masses when duty called."[13]

The regime's intent was clear: it would menace Africans with genocidal rhetoric, banish activists, and obliterate dissent. Facing this onslaught, ANC leaders asked whether civil disobedience could effect change. Luthuli continued to support nonviolence, organizing pass-burning demonstrations and announcing a Stay at Home campaign to climax in a "Day of Mourning and Protest." Nokukhanya participated in a five-day fast to protest the state of emergency. The government reacted to all this by incarcerating Albert for five months, convicting him of pass burning.[14] Cell guards beat Luthuli, who was then suffering from a coronary thrombosis and high blood pressure. He spent the last months of his detention in a prison hospital.[15] With the president-general out of commission, Mandela gained influence in the ANC.[16] During the state of emergency, which lasted from March to August 1960, Mandela and communist African ANC members Sisulu and Nokwe, along with white communists Joe Slovo and Rusty Bernstein, mapped a course to revolution. Meanwhile, communists Dadoo, Kotane, Turok, and Michael Harmel, amongst the few in the Congress Alliance who avoided arrest, became de facto ANC leaders, operating underground in a tightly organized cell.[17] Luthuli was privy to neither the ambitions nor the itineraries of these two groups. In July 1960, SACP members and London-based South African exiles Yusuf Dadoo and Vella Pillay met Russian leaders in Moscow with the aim of advancing insurrection in South Africa. In late October and early November, Dadoo and Pillay were in China for weapons and logistics training. By that November, ANC-SACP member Joe Matthews and SACP member Michael Harmel traveled from South Africa to Moscow, where they joined Dadoo and Pillay to attend the International Meeting of the Communist and Workers' Parties in November 1960.[18] During the December 1960 SACP national conference, attendees, including Mandela, Sisulu, Mbeki, Kotane, and Raymond Mhlaba, agreed to pursue an unspecified form of armed struggle.[19] Against Stephen Ellis's explosive charge that the SACP was a Soviet puppet directing the ANC to armed struggle, Paul Landau and Thula Simpson persuasively suggest otherwise, positing that, while Mandela and his comrades appreciated Eastern Bloc attention, they orchestrated their own self-defense plan that had a long genesis from at least the early 1950s.[20]

But Mandela understood that it would be difficult to sell the military option, "particularly to Luthuli,"[21] who in the meantime had helped organize a December 1960 conference in Orlando, outside of Johannesburg, that brought together 36 different organizations to establish a united front against the government. Though Luthuli's banning orders prevented him from attending, he later proposed a new national constitution that protected all South Africans and mass demonstrations against what would soon be declared the Republic of South Africa. The forum for discussing these initiatives was an All-In African conference in Pietermaritzburg. When it commenced on March 25, 1961, Luthuli was upstaged by Mandela's return from the underground and his appearance before the conference. The possibility of peaceful international intervention seemed less likely when, in April 1961, the UN Security Council refused to ratify a General Assembly Resolution proclaiming apartheid "a flagrant violation of . . . the Universal Declaration of Human Rights."[22] Meanwhile, Pretoria repudiated pressure for reform from Commonwealth nations by becoming an independent republic on May 31, 1961. This was a victory for Verwoerd; after Sharpeville, he had survived a bullet fired point-blank at his face by a white assassin and had managed to stabilize an economy reeling from massive capital outflows.[23]

On the heels of the All-In initiative, the regime arrested ten thousand Africans, stationed troops in townships, and disrupted a strike denouncing the South African Republic. Mandela warned the state that unleashing "naked force [on] our non-violent struggle" would end "a chapter . . . of a non-violent policy." He ruffled the NEC, which never authorized this fiery caveat.[24] Interestingly, Tambo, charged with establishing the ANC external mission, declared in a London speech that if the government crushed the strike "it would be the last time the ANC would talk of peace."[25] Mandela labeled apartheid a cancer with one therapy, his words reminiscent of Frantz Fanon's cathartic remedy for pernicious colonialism. "At the level of individuals," Fanon wrote in *Wretched of the Earth*, "violence is a cleansing force . . . [because it] frees the native from his inferiority complex . . . makes him fearless and restores his self-respect. Even if the armed struggle has been symbolic . . . the people have the time to see that the liberation has been the business of each and all."[26] With Mpondoland insurgents seeking weapons from the ANC to combat Bantu Authorities, women and youth in townships such as Cato Manor attacking apartheid structures, and groups such as the SACP, PAC, the National Liberation Movement Committee, and the Yu Chi Chan Club contemplating war, nonviolence in South Africa seemed to have run its course.[27] Though the 1950s had been the high point of the nonviolent civil disobedience strategies led by Luthuli, Mandela now believed it was time for the ANC to command an armed struggle.

The 1961 Meetings and the Birth of Umkhonto we Sizwe

Between 1961 and 1962, the "internal security" panic gripped South Africa. The PAC threatened civil war. Police and army units acted in concert, reinforcing repression. Luthuli doubted "whether anything but indiscriminate bloodshed and violence will make any impression. . . . If the whites continue as at present, nobody will give the signal for mass violence. Nobody will need to."[28] At the dawn of African decolonization, Luthuli stated that Pretoria was bent on "concentration camps, terrorism, and legalized murder."[29] Was it useful to espouse civil disobedience, he may have wondered, in the face of unceasing detentions, government massacres, and treason trials? Could he rely on the West to see through Pretoria's Cold War propaganda demonizing the ANC as godless communists?[30] Could he expect Christian allies in the United States and Great Britain to stop "deadly" Afrikaner nationalism? Luthuli had compared "concentration camp" apartheid to a fatal force bent on its own final solution. Could he continue to pray for divine peace to save his people from racist hell?[31]

During a session of the NEC Working Group in June 1961, Mandela urged the ANC to adopt a self-defense platform. Unnerved, Kotane rejected this option because it "exposed innocent people to massacres by the enemy."[32] Shortly afterwards, Mandela appealed privately to Kotane with a Sesotho axiom, "Sebatana ha se bokwe ka diatla" (Attacks of the wild beast cannot be averted with only bare hands).[33] Mandela argued that the government's bans on the ANC and nonviolent protest had changed the calculus; the ANC could not wait for Leninist conditions (favored by the communist Kotane) to arise as they did in 1917 Bolshevik Russia. Rather, the ANC had to expand and adapt its strategies in the new underground conditions and draw inspiration from armed insurrections in Algeria, Vietnam, and especially Cuba, where bush guerrillas drilled by Fidel Castro and Che Guevara had toppled Fulgencio Batista's regime. Mandela argued that of all antiapartheid groups, only the ANC had the capacity to successfully adopt armed struggle and warned that if the ANC did not lead in this new direction, they would fall hopelessly behind their own movement. A skeptical Kotane nevertheless allowed Mandela to present his proposal at the next Working Group session, ultimately authorizing the idea of self-defense to be tabled at a NEC meeting scheduled for the following month outside Durban.[34] In advance of these deliberations, Mandela and Kotane huddled separately with Luthuli. Mandela coveted the president-general's "blessing," but Luthuli "could not publicly support an armed struggle," though he added crucially that he "would not oppose it."[35] The Cape Town–based activist Amy Rietstein chronicled these developments. She visited Wolfie Kodesh's flat in Johannesburg, where Mandela hid from police. During her stay, Rietstein typed Mandela's NEC report making the case for self-defense, which he presented to Luthuli. Unable to restrain Mandela, the president-general solicited Kotane's opinion.[36]

As Luthuli's influence over his movement waned, his posture toward violence evolved. Charles Hooper, who introduced the 1962 edition of Luthuli's autobiography *Let My People Go*, registered this modifying attitude. Between 1957 and 1960, Hooper interviewed the "Chief" more than a dozen times. During their exchanges, Luthuli emphasized the appropriateness of "morally defensible" aggression—for instance, when "a madman [is] attacking one's family." Hooper described Luthuli's "condemnation of violence . . . [as] conditional and qualified" in the face of "pass arrest, night raids, 180 days [detention], and the starvation of minds and bodies." If the ANC acquired weapons, Luthuli exhorted, its arsenal should be "employed massively with a real chance of success; or with restraint as the final means of trying to warn of trouble ahead, and then against installations, not people." In these scenarios, he imagined "that no violent course," if mapped, was either "predictable or controllable."[37] His close friend Goolam Suleiman described Luthuli as "a very humble person" who "wouldn't harm a fly" but recalled the Chief saying, "There may come a time when we have to use violence—when violence will be forced on us."[38] Luthuli also told his secretary and biographer Mary Benson, "the leadership stand by the non-violent method." Nevertheless, he considered whether "these white men taking advantage of our seeming docility" would propel "some, particularly young people[,] . . . to question the efficacy of non-violence when they face so aggressive a Government." He opined, "if the oppressed people here ever came to indulge in violent ways . . . however much you may disagree with them, you cannot blame them."[39]

In July 1961, the ANC and the Congress Alliance

allies met near Groutville, expressly so the banned Luthuli could preside over pivotal debates about armed struggle. The NEC session convened in July 1961 on the Stanger farm of Walter Singh, where Luthuli, Yengwa, and approximately sixty people debated Mandela's armed self-defense proposals. There was some pressure to come to consensus since a Joint Congress Alliance meeting was scheduled for the next evening. Also, some participants may have been aware that the SACP was forming military units for sabotage operations; they would soon go to China for military training.[40] Luthuli's inclusive, democratic leadership set the tone for the collective decision-making in the ANC NEC and Congress Alliance meetings over the next two nights. Early on in the NEC meeting, Luthuli stated his opposition to armed struggle. Beyond his own personal preference for continued nonviolent action, on a practical level, Luthuli knew that during the long and just-completed Treason Trial, he and numerous other ANC leaders had affirmed the organization's nonviolent principles. He also certainly understood that his members could not win a war when they lacked both modern firearms and any experience of a modern battlefield. Indeed, Mandela himself had never fired a gun. Finally, as ANC president, it would have been highly undemocratic leadership to unilaterally adopt armed struggle as official ANC policy; a shift that would betray the rank and file, which adhered to foundational rules requiring a national conference to transform ANC policy. There was also a desire to protect not only ANC members but also still-legal Congress Alliance partners from likely state retribution.[41]

Mandela recalled that "we worked on" Luthuli "the whole night and I think that in his heart he realized we were right. He ultimately agreed that a military campaign was inevitable."[42] Still unconvinced of the need for counterviolence, Yengwa contributed to the "searching debate." His view of the Stanger proceedings illuminates the shared acceptance of armed struggle and Luthuli's reluctant accord with Mandela's "logic."[43] Other participants in "these discussions," such as Curnick Ndlovu, thought that Luthuli "believed unquestionably in non-violent struggle" but "he was not a leader who believed in dictating. . . . The ANC had stood the test of time because of collective leadership." Joe Matthews, too, noted how the president-general's insistence on nonviolence gave way to compromise.[44] According to Mandela, Luthuli himself suggested "two separate streams of the struggle": the ANC, which would remain nonviolent; and a "military movement [that] should be a separate and independent organ, linked to the ANC and under the overall control of the ANC, but fundamentally autonomous."[45] This compromise would permit the creation of a distinct sabotage unit that hit hard targets. Meanwhile, meeting at a different location in preparation for the Congress Alliance meeting the next night, there were also divergent opinions within the unbanned Natal Indian Congress, with some members supporting nonviolent principles, while others advocated counterviolence.[46]

The ensuing night Luthuli chaired an ANC-led gathering of the Joint Congress Alliance in a beach house near Stanger. Members of the ANC, SAIC, SACTU, FEDSAW, CPC, and COD filled the venue. The president-general opened the assembly by recognizing MK, but demonstrating his democratic, inclusive style, he stipulated that MK discussions begin anew with Congress allies present. Mandela recalled Luthuli's feeling that armed self-defense was "a matter of such gravity, I would like my colleagues here tonight to consider the issue afresh." Thus, the armed-struggle debate was rekindled, to the dismay of Mandela. Ismail Meer chronicled the contentious back-and-forth, which "contemplated . . . violence as an easy way out of the hard task of mobilizing the people in the face of repression" and promoted "violent means" to harness "rising militancy."[47] Luthuli mediated different proposals, such as a nationwide strike; this motion prompted a complaint from the floor that the ANC was shying from a physical fight. Apparently, the president-general retorted, "If anybody thinks I'm a pacifist, let him go and take my chickens, he will know how wrong he is!"[48] Sisulu recalled that the Zulu "Chief [who] . . . was a great admirer of Shaka and . . . not opposed to violence in principle" was proffering an "argument . . . that all forms of struggle were not exhausted."[49] SAIC chairperson and Ghandian disciple Dr. Monty Naicker backed this line, with J. N. Singh clarifying that "non-violence has not failed us, we have failed non-violence." Mandela chimed in, proclaiming that passive resistance had not halted apartheid repression.[50] Following Mandela, NIC member Yusuf Cachalia cautioned that counterviolence would provoke the state to "arrest us . . . [and] slaughter us." M. D. Naidoo dissented, accusing some NIC colleagues of being afraid, a charge that instigated recriminations.[51]

The stalemate ground on until Kotane broke the impasse by asking for the authorization of a self-defense option. He advised MK "not [to] involve us" as "the policy of non-violence . . . can only be changed by the National Executive," and instructed Mandela to "coordinate with others that are in the field . . . [and to] keep on reporting."[52] In the light of dawn, Alliance members, some with optimism and others with disquiet, agreed to these stipulations and certified the prior decision taken at Singh's farm.[53] Luthuli, Kotane, and Naicker were instrumental in devising the dual resolution to uphold nonviolence while sanctioning the establishment of an affiliated sabotage wing: "You go and start that organization. We will not discipline you because we understand the conditions under which you have taken this line. But . . . we [the ANC] are going to continue with nonviolence."[54] This statement acknowledged the double bind in which circumstances had placed the ANC. Only a majority of the organization's delegates polled at a national conference could formalize armed struggle, but since the movement was banned, this conference was all but impossible. Against lingering notions that Luthuli had no knowledge of MK's formation, Kader Asmal claimed knowledge that "plans for an armed struggle, under the auspices of a new military formation, were submitted to Chief Luthuli for his approval."[55] But MK sabotage was to be supplemental to ongoing political action and aim to cripple the national economy without collateral bloodshed, raise wider awareness of apartheid intransigence, and force a shaken government to the negotiating table.[56]

There is no extant evidence of Luthuli ever repudiating the formation of MK. On the contrary, his avowal not to "countenance . . . loss of life" was affirmed by Mandela's explanation of what could be carried out: "forays against military installations, power plants . . . and transportation links."[57] At this time, Luthuli and Kotane showed no inclination to support Mandela's evocations of guerrilla warfare.[58] While Luthuli remained troubled by the prospect of armed struggle escalating the existential threat of a racial Armageddon, pacifism was not his answer either.[59] After being kept abreast of MK developments by Kotane and Natal MK leader Curnick Ndlovu, Luthuli was said to have remarked, "Look, I am not a communist . . . but that doesn't mean that when I am attacked, I will just be like Christ and turn the other cheek. I will fight back. MK is a way of fighting back . . . [but what] I would like you not to do is to say that MK is officially an ANC body."[60] MK became part of a generalized turn to armed struggle in southern Africa, with similar military units founded in South Africa, Angola, South West Africa, Mozambique, and Southern Rhodesia in the early 1960s.

The Nobel Peace Prize

To Pretoria's consternation, on October 23, 1961, Luthuli became the first African-born recipient of the Nobel Peace Prize and the first ever to win in the new category of Human Rights. The award propelled him from backwater obscurity to global celebrity.[61] Congratulatory letters poured in, including telexes from American president John F. Kennedy and the heads of twenty-five different countries.[62] Descending on Groutville, journalists lined up to interview the new laureate; their dispatches recorded Luthuli's gratitude to Nokukhanya, "with whom I share common ideals and values," and his belief that the award belonged, above all, to the ANC and its antiapartheid crusade. Luthuli immediately sensed that he had a global podium from which to address "our suffering and humiliation." Through the press, he enjoined the UN and South Africa's top trading partners to impose embargoes on Verwoerd's regime.[63] Probably with the recent MK decision on his mind, Luthuli stressed the urgency of the moment; "events are moving fast," he intoned ominously; "the time is a few minutes to 12."[64] At joyous rallies, thousands of Luthuli's supporters sang "Nkosi Sikelel' iAfrika" (God bless Africa) and "Somlandela Luthuli" and cheered Yengwa's *izibongo* (Zulu praise song): "the

Albert and Nokuhanya Luthuli feeding their chickens at home, 1961. (Bailey's African History Archives, photograph by Drum Photographer)

great bull that enemies tried to fence in a kraal has broken the strong fence and wandered far, as far as Oslo! Chief of Groutville! Chief of Africa!"[65]

Some whites, including parliamentarian Jan Steytler and the Pietermaritzburg City Council, congratulated Luthuli, and the white-run newspaper the *Natal Daily News* feted him as "a man with moral and intellectual qualities that have earned him the respect of the world and a position of leadership" and urged the government to "listen to the voice of responsible African opinion."[66] Famed South African author and Liberal Party leader Alan Paton concluded that Luthuli was "the only man in South Africa who could lead both the left and the right, both the moderns and the traditionalists, both Africans and non-Africans."[67] But state officials and hostile newspaper articles claimed that the award was a malicious attempt to embarrass South Africa and that Luthuli was as undeserving of the Nobel Prize as Adolf Hitler—a rich irony, given the widespread right-wing admiration of the Nazi leader. The government-controlled South African Broadcasting Company (SABC) broadcast a defamatory radio program about Luthuli, and Minister of the Interior Jan de Klerk initially refused to issue Luthuli a passport to travel to Oslo. This was no idle threat, since Luthuli was already "a prisoner in my own land": earlier in 1961, the government had twice refused to allow him to travel to the Eastern Cape to accept the Christopher Gell Award for his activism.[68] After intense domestic and international pressure, the government finally issued a passport, but declared bitterly that Luthuli's honor had "debased" the Nobel and was not "based on merit, but instead to further propaganda objectives, which must necessarily rob the Nobel Peace Award of all its high esteem." They also refused Luthuli's request to attend Tanganyika's independence ceremonies en route to Oslo.[69]

As they made their way out of South Africa, Nokukhanya marveled at "those crowds" in Durban and Johannesburg.[70] During a brief London stopover, they were reunited with Tambo and Duma Nokwe, leaders of the new ANC external mission, and also met with the deeply committed Christian antiapartheid leaders Canon John Collins and Trevor Huddleston. In Oslo,

Albert and Nokukhanya Luthuli feted at Oslo, Norway, December 1961. (Keystone USA via ZUMAPRESS.com)

reporters asked about rumors of imminent racial war in South Africa. After reiterating the ANC policy of nonviolence, Luthuli responded with rhetoric ostensibly aimed at MK. Armed resistance was political suicide since it would give the state a tailor-made excuse to engage its massive arsenal of weapons in a genocidal slaughter of South African blacks. He vowed, "I would never lead my people into a situation where they would be mowed down." Making a subtle but important distinction between the ANC and MK, the president-general also remarked, "There are no responsible persons among us in the ANC who advocate violence as a means of furthering our cause." He asked rhetorically, "What do you get out of violence, except that you increase the chances of bitterness, and are you more likely to effect violence to reach an end? I say no."[71] Privately, he confided a different sentiment to his friend Mary-Louise Hooper in Norway. "There can be no real peace," Luthuli postulated, "as long as people are oppressed."[72] He reportedly disclosed to one Nobel dignitary that he "felt bound at a meeting with the ANC's leaders some months earlier to accept a decision to embark on sabotage."[73] Ominously, in November 1961, ANC allies, the South African Congress of Democrats, South African Congress of Trade Unions, South African Indian Congress, and South African Coloured People's Congress, issued a statement warning that there would be no further tolerance of "peace in bondage" and vowed to "summon all our brain and brawn" to fight apartheid oppression.[74]

For Mandela, Sisulu, and other exponents of armed struggle, Luthuli's honor came at the wrong time. If Luthuli's clock showed "a few minutes to twelve," by their reckoning it was already three minutes past midnight. Adulatory English-language coverage of the Nobel announcement clouded Luthuli's status as well; militants outside the ANC, including the PAC,

114

pointed to the "peace prize" headlines when deriding his organization as a liberal front hailed by European paternalists. Neville Alexander, of the Yu Chi Chan Club, later scorned Luthuli as a "patsy of the white man."[75] Chief Luthuli had never been anyone's patsy, as he was a man whom his close friend E. V. Mohamed proclaimed had "fire in his belly."[76] Throughout his political life, he had been valued for his integrity and courage. Never an ideologue, he had always shown an empathetic awareness and clarity about the different strands and energies that made up his resistance movement. Before Mandela's emergence, Luthuli seemed to represent the African leader most capable of holding a national movement together in diverse South Africa. He

Albert Luthuli receiving the Nobel Peace Prize, December 1961. (Keystone USA via ZUMAPRESS.com)

had shown a remarkable ability to resolve the contradictions that threatened to tear the movement apart. Now, in a moment of global recognition of what he had fought to achieve, he could no longer overcome the tensions swirling around him. He could only live the contradictions that he had understood more fully, perhaps, than anyone else.

Wearing the *iziqu* necklace of Zulu warriors "who had killed in battle," on December 10, 1961, Luthuli entered Oslo City Hall, where a convocation awaited the conferral of his medal.[77] Shortly thereafter, he delivered a lecture saluting "disciplined resistance" in South Africa. Luthuli exposed Verwoerd's decolonization language of "trusteeship," "separate development," "race federation," and "partnership" as rhetorical devices that obscured the fundamentally fascist apartheid state, a relic of the dark ages, born from legacies of slavery and colonialism.[78] In stark contrast to the civil religion of white supremacy "worshipped like a god" in South Africa, Luthuli praised those Christians who condemned apartheid as antithetical to the teachings of Jesus Christ. He ended his speech on an ominous note, reciting Revelation 6:9–12, verses that promised an apocalypse that would create a just and peaceful kingdom. In a line that Luthuli decided to omit when he delivered the speech, COD member Rusty Bernstein, who had helped in drafting the speech, noted the irony that this honor coincided with the end of fifty years of ANC nonviolence. Bernstein reflected later in his memoir, "Non-violence had always been a hard course to steer in a violent country.

. . . Yesterday's non-violent ANC had spawned today's armed liberation force."[79]

South African government officials responded to Luthuli's sharp criticisms with veiled threats of retribution, but Luthuli decided not to follow Tambo into exile. "No, the struggle is here. I can't go."[80] This decision was pivotal. Luthuli was at the apex of his global renown, well positioned, with his impressive statesmanship, to lead the ANC external mission and a nascent global antiapartheid movement from abroad. Instead, he returned to an isolated, lonely existence in Groutville, punished ever more severely by a vengeful state bent on imprisoning him in the land of his birth, even refusing permission for his non-African friends to enter Groutville, an African reserve, to attend his daughter Albertina's wedding the following month. The mantle of leadership would soon pass to younger leaders such as Mandela and Tambo. With Luthuli in Oslo, Mandela accelerated MK plans. At this juncture he was more excited by Algerian attacks on French colonists than by Luthuli's moment.[81] Moreover, MK was eager to eclipse rivals in the South African field. The first ANC saboteurs knew that the Liberal Party offshoot National Committee of Liberation (later the African Resistance Movement) had already conducted over twenty successful sabotage attempts in the last few months and that POQO, the PAC's armed wing, was promising to win freedom through violence "by January 1."[82]

Luthuli and MK: "I Understand These Fellows Fully"

> It is easy enough for those who possess the
> privilege of freedom to call for restraint and
> patience on the part of those who have no
> such privilege; but not so easy for the victims
> of apartheid.
>
> —Reverend Canon L. John Collins[83]

As the Luthulis returned to Durban on the evening of
December 15, MK began operations in that city.[84] Luthuli had no involvement, but according to Natal MK
leader Billy Nair, he had prior knowledge of MK's launch.
Nair later remembered that Luthuli "already knew,
before he left for Oslo, to receive the Nobel, he knew
that night, that Umkhonto was going to be launched."[85]
MK launched similar attacks in Johannesburg and Port
Elizabeth on December 16. Echoing Luthuli's words to
Kotane, Sisulu called his saboteurs a "fighting arm" of
the liberation movement. The devices were planted outside vacant government offices and around remote state
assets, such as transmission lines. This maiden mission
had more failures than successes. Some explosives were
duds; one operative was accidentally blown up. Still,
six blasts shook cities, with each detonation announcing MK's declaration that "the government policy of
force, suppression, and violence will no longer be met
with non-violent resistance only."[86] The December 16
offensive disrupted a national holiday, when Afrikaners
commemorated their defeat of "savage" Zulu regiments

at "Blood River" in 1838, while Africans lamented the loss of King Dingane's army in a battle to repulse Boer invaders.[87]

While Luthuli recognized that the calculus of liberation had changed, he still hoped that nonviolence would win the day after his Peace Prize and the emergence of a dynamic antiapartheid Afro-Asian bloc at the UN. Questioned days later by the press, Luthuli expressed "regret" and denied knowing who was responsible for the explosions.[88] He knew that the response of "white supremacists" to African resistance was to "bring out the guns and the other techniques of intimidation and present themselves as restorers of order."[89] He now sought additional information from his organization, and MK leader Curnick Ndlovu was dispatched from the underground "Rivonia" base to Luthuli. They discussed the distribution of flyers broadcasting reasons for the bombings. Luthuli said "he was not aware that the [MK] leaflet was coming . . . [but] was not opposed to it . . . [nor] the feeling."[90] He also summoned Kotane. In one of their exchanges, Luthuli used an allegory to illustrate a crisis between the ANC guardian and his assertive children: "When my son decides to sleep with a girl, he does not ask for my permission, but just does it. It is only afterwards, when the girl is pregnant and the parents make a case, that he brings his troubles home."[91] Yet this rift, Yengwa recalled, did not shake Luthuli's "outspoken" affirmation of "the young men . . . Mandela and the other leaders . . . driven to commit acts of sabotage, because of the government oppressing the . . . liberation movement."[92]

Luthuli's American-born confidant John Reuling, a former teacher at Adams who was invited to the Nobel ceremonies, recorded similar sentiments. Eluding police in January 1962, Reuling visited Groutville, where he and the laureate walked into a sugar field to whisper behind a screen of cane stalks. Reuling noted Luthuli's compassion for "the young fellows [who] come to me and say, 'You have been non-violent for these many years, and this law has passed, and there are these many more people in prison, these many more people in detention, and this trial and that trial and we simply can't see the way out except by . . . fighting.'" Luthuli added, "5 or 10 years ago I would have told them they are going down the wrong track—now I just don't know. . . . I understand these fellows fully, and I simply cannot blame them."[93] Jordan Ngubane plumbed the dilemma of "nonviolence . . . in South Africa," where there was no "freedom to assemble or to travel, [or mobilize] a large army of disciplined volunteers," as "the police can trace the movements of a person virtually from day to day." Since "Sharpeville showed so clearly that mass nonviolence leads to shootings," he detected no "enthusiasm among the Africans for" entering the arena of civil disobedience to "lose."[94] Ngubane thus alluded to Luthuli's motivation to link "battles . . . of Tshaka . . . Gandhi" to the sacrifices of "martyrs who fell at Sharpeville . . . Pondoland . . . and Sekhukuneland."[95] So while Luthuli publicly extolled peaceful Christianity, for example in his column for the *Golden City Post*, he pondered defensive tactics within a continuum marked by the poles of nonviolence and violence.

On January 3, 1962, Luthuli met with colleagues to review Minister of Justice John Vorster's sabotage bill, which allowed a maximum sentence of death for sabotage. Luthuli disapproved of the bombers' handbills declaring nonviolence "dead" and MK's association with the ANC.[96] The group heard him out and opted to grant saboteurs autonomy under joint purview of the ANC and the SACP. Although dismayed by the timing of MK's debut, Luthuli never resigned from his movement, as he had threatened to do years earlier when accused of being afraid of whites.[97] Instead, he strengthened cooperation with national branches and ANC offices elsewhere on the continent, and approved NEC orders for Mandela to participate in the February 1962 Pan-African Freedom Movement for East Central Africa (PAFMECA) in Ethiopia, which offered "military training."[98] On January 8, 1962, Mandela convened with Luthuli in Groutville, where the latter protested MK's launch but did not oppose its formation; they talked, as well, about gaining allies during Mandela's upcoming African tour, an expedition that he embarked upon without a passport.[99]

In May or June 1962, Luthuli gathered close to home with Kotane, Sisulu, and MK personnel Ndlovu, Ronnie Kasrils, and Billy Nair present. The tightening dragnet of the security state, Mandela's reconnaissance, and Tambo's pursuits topped the agenda. In July 1962, parliament passed the General Law Amendment Act (No. 76), which broadened the definition of sabotage to encompass labor strikes and political graffiti. It also reversed the burden of proof for those accused of deliberately damaging government property: if found guilty, they could be executed. ANC members regarded the legislation as an act of war. After his return to South Africa in early August, clad in fatigues, MK's commander-in-chief, Mandela, quietly entered Groutville to brief the president-general. When Mandela noted that African leaders had reservations about the presence of communists and non-Africans within the Congress Alliance, and argued that the ANC needed to project a more overt African nationalism to gain needed continental support, Luthuli "did not like the idea of foreign politicians dictating policy to the ANC . . . [declining to] alter our policy because it did not suit a few foreign leaders." After debriefing Luthuli, Mandela unwisely reveled with friends at a nearby party; word leaked that he was in Luthuli's vicinity. Acting on a tip from the U.S. Central Intelligence Agency, which spied on liberation movements in southern Africa, South African police captured Mandela on August 5 near the Natal town of Howick. He would be charged with not having secured a permit to leave the country.[100]

The ANC now confronted "a very dangerous situation," Joe Matthews recalled, as even former ANC secretary-general James Calata, referring to MK, asked Z. K. Matthews, "Intoni le High Command?" (What is this High Command?). Other members wondered, "Which political organization established the military body?" During October 1962, the ANC leaders Govan Mbeki, Sisulu, Tambo, Kotane, and Yengwa—but not the banned Luthuli, who could not attend—were part of an ANC consultative conference in neighboring Lobatse, Bechuanaland Protectorate, that formally linked the ANC and MK and transferred effective power to ANC vice president Tambo, head of the ANC external mission.[101] Luthuli's reaction to these momentous shifts remains unknown, though his future actions indicate that he handled these changes with grace and magnanimity.[102] Publicizing the Lobatse decision in April 1963, the ANC and its allies lamented that intensified government repression, including indefinite detention, ever more sadistic forms of torture, and mass executions, had made "violence . . . the keynote . . . in South Africa. The government is frantically arming itself."[103] Inspired by the Cuban and Algerian examples of revolutionary violence, MK vowed to "take the gloves off."[104] By June 1963, MK had conducted over two hundred operations. But in July 1963, with Mandela starting to serve his five-year prison term, police raided a farm in Rivonia, a suburb of Johannesburg; the property, known as Lilliesleaf, concealed MK principals mulling over Operation Mayibuye, a blueprint for guerrilla warfare.[105] Seven suspects were taken into custody with weapons and materials implicating Mandela. He would stand trial again, this time for sedition, alongside the Rivonia defendants. The prospect that a conviction would send these ANC men to the gallows agitated and "depressed" Luthuli.[106] On August 28, 1963, the Durban-based British consul-general Anthony Eden interviewed the chief. The day before, Verwoerd had delivered a bellicose speech in Natal glorying in "white unity." Such racist triumphalism, according to Eden's transcript, provoked Luthuli to say that "he would use violence in the last resort, and this time has probably come."[107]

"Just, Brave Men" and International Nonviolence

In this bleak milieu Luthuli coordinated antiapartheid protests with the ACOA and the UN Special Committee Against Apartheid, steered by Enuga Reddy, which fostered boycotts of South Africa.[108] By September 1962, the Reverend Martin Luther King Jr.—an admirer of the president-general, ACOA, and the UN, had kicked off the U.S. Appeal for Action against Apartheid. Boosted by this solidarity, Luthuli beseeched the world to recognize that the ANC had "been forced to abandon all hope of reaching a just solution by consultation and negotiation."[109] Calling for weapon embargoes and trade boycotts, particularly by Britain, South Africa's largest trading partner, Luthuli communicated with external ANC leaders Oliver Tambo and Robert Resha.[110] With the death penalty looming for the Rivonia defendants, Luthuli implored British diplomats and the UN secretary-general in March 1964 to "save the lives of the nine ... [ANC] leaders."[111] "With them will be interred this country's hopes," he lamented. Luthuli took comfort in their "spirit of militancy," which embodied "the highest in morality and ethics." It was not easy, he professed, for his organization to pursue "justice by the use of violent methods," but the "uncompromising white refusal to" ensure "freedom" for "the African and other oppressed" pushed the ANC in this direction.[112] His advocacy was part of the successful effort by the UN's Afro-Asian bloc to put forward what became Resolution 182, calling for an arms embargo against South Africa and demanding the release of imprisoned antiapartheid activists, passed by the UN Security Council on December 4, 1963. Reflecting considerable international pressure on South Africa not to execute the Rivonia trialists, on June 9, 1964, the UN Security Council passed Resolution 190, which called for the trial's end and a disavowal of the death penalty.

On June 11, 1964, before trial judge Quartus de Wet rendered his decision, outside the courthouse two thousand Africans demonstrated for the defendants' release while a few white students from the University of Pretoria demanded conviction and the death penalty. Judge de Wet convicted all but two of the Rivonia trialists of all charges, an unsurprising verdict given the clear evidence of sabotage. But would the convicted men be sentenced to the death penalty or life imprisonment? In a hushed courtroom, and with trembling hands and a virtually inaudible voice, Judge de Wet imposed life sentences on the convicted men. We may never know if Judge de Wet was influenced by the prospect that a death sentence could spark international sanctions against South Africa, as well as be a public relations nightmare for its Western allies.[113] Perhaps, he reasoned, life imprisonment would have the same practical effect as the death penalty, permanently removing the Rivonia trialists from South African politics, while avoiding the martyrdom and the international backlash that a death sentence could provoke. Whatever de Wet's reasoning, no one, including the Rivonia trialists, expected that one day they would be free.

That same day, Luthuli issued a statement of support for the sentenced men, who he felt represented "the highest in morality and ethics in the South African political struggle." Noting that the ANC's long history "of a militant, nonviolent struggle" had been met by white intransigence, Luthuli declared, "no one can blame brave just men for seeking justice by the use of violent methods; nor could they be blamed if they tried to create an organized force in order to ultimately establish peace and racial harmony." He called for the United States and Great Britain, South Africa's most powerful trading partners and allies, to lead an international sanctions movement that would "save these men [and] what they stand for," to end apartheid and avoid what could be "the greatest African tragedy of our times."[114]

Luthuli at his Groutville grocery shop, 1964. (Bailey's African History Archives, Photograph by Ranjith Kally)

Luthuli's international nonviolence had support from his friend and fellow antiapartheid crusader Martin Luther King Jr. Before he had any idea he would win the Nobel Prize himself, King had prayed for the "Beloved Community" of antiracists to aid the ANC. En route to the 1964 Oslo ceremony to accept his prize, he stopped in London to give an "Address on South African Independence." In the audience sat citizens of Luthuli's continent, Luthuli's exiled compatriots, and human rights advocates from India, Pakistan, the West Indies, and the United States. King connected the global color line from America to South Africa: "Clearly there is much in Mississippi and Alabama to remind South Africans of their own country." He praised "Chief Luthuli for his leadership" and identified "with those in the far more deadly struggle" who "strove for half a century to win ... by non-violent methods" before "the shootings of Sharpeville and all that has happened since."[115] Rivonia convinced King that peaceful demonstrations only produced "years of punishment for Mandela" along with "hundreds wasting away in Robben Island." King predicted that if the United States and Great Britain, particularly, were to withdraw all economic investments and trade from South Africa, "then apartheid would be brought to an end," allowing "South Africans of all races [to] ... build the shared society they desire."[116]

On December 10, 1964, King's Nobel Peace Prize acceptance speech included a parable about "the dedicated pilots of our struggle," such as Albert Luthuli, "who have sat at the controls as the freedom movement soared into orbit," despite being "met with the most brutal expression of man's inhumanity to man." King, too, distinguished the right of freedom seekers to repel their oppressors.[117] He and Luthuli, two laureates confronting variants of transnational racism, had merged forces through the ACOA. This organization provided a pulpit for King's critique of Pretoria's "white supremacy," in which he demanded "Let My People Go" to combat "a medieval segregation . . . organized with twentieth-century efficiency and drive." Likening apartheid to "a sophisticated form of slavery," King pondered, "Have we the power to be more than peevish with South Africa, but yet refrain from acts of war?"[118] Both King and Luthuli shared a gospel of service to God and oppressed people everywhere, evoking Exodus 9:1 in which God used Moses as his messenger to tell Pharaoh, "Let my people go, so that they may worship me." But would the modern-day Pharaohs ever let their people go?

Death by a Thousand Cuts

As the Sabotage Act further shackled Luthuli, the young Coloured artist Ronald Harrison unveiled a remarkable painting entitled *The Black Christ* that portrayed Luthuli, representing suffering black South Africans, as a modern-day Christ persecuted by apartheid's ideologues Verwoerd and Vorster, cast as modern-day embodiments of the Roman centurions who tortured Christ. Surrounded by an Asian St. John and a Coloured Madonna, along with depictions of state repression and antiapartheid resistance, the portrait captured both the perils and promise of South Africa. Harrison explained his choice of Luthuli: "I could think of no other African in whom I had found my perfect image of Christ I would like to see in the life hereafter."[119] After a brief public exhibition in Cape Town in August 1962, the apartheid regime banned the *The Black Christ* and Harrison wisely smuggled the painting to London.[120] Utilizing clauses in the 1962 Sabotage Act and charging that Luthuli's activities "furthered Communism," Minister of Justice John Vorster placed Luthuli under house arrest with a new five-year ban, effective May 31, 1964.[121] Luthuli could not accept speaking engagements or receive human rights awards abroad, and could not even attend his nearby church. He became increasingly isolated from the ANC, itself driven underground and struggling to maintain a viable presence in the repressive police state.[122] Luthuli still managed to transmit his message to the world through visitors such as American journalist Studs Terkel and U.S. senator Robert F. Kennedy, who, during his 1966 South African tour, made the pilgrimage to Groutville after addressing the South African Parliament in Cape Town. The two men discussed the American civil rights and the South African antiapartheid struggles, and the inspired Kennedy subsequently led a Durban crowd in a stirring rendition of the civil rights anthem "We Shall Overcome." The senator praised Luthuli as "one of the most impressive men that I have ever met."[123]

United States Senator Robert F. Kennedy visits Luthuli, monitored by South African security police, June 1966. Kennedy later described Luthuli "as one of the most impressive men I have met." (Getty)

But when the dignitaries departed, police harassment intensified, with frequent house raids that made Luthuli "very touchy" and "depressed." Nokukhanya recalled, "they used to come and fetch him from home. Sometimes without notice, they would take him away, talking to him about stopping what he was doing. They wanted him to resign from the ANC. That was the main thing. They would talk and talk to him and bring him back in the evening."[124] Luthuli's 1964 ban prevented treatment by his Durban-based doctor, D. A. Edington, a supposed communist. His medical history already included a heart attack and strokes, and he suffered from chronic high blood pressure. Now a concerned Nokukhanya told Mary-Louise Hooper of her husband's "marked deterioration." Hooper publicized this dire situation during her October 29, 1964, special hearing with the UN Special Committee Against Apartheid. International pressure forced the government to relax Luthuli's ban, including travel to Durban to receive treatment from Edington, who recorded that Luthuli now suffered from blindness in his left eye.[125] Under house arrest and with Nokukhanya spending several months each year tending to Swaziland farms bought with Nobel Peace Prize money, Luthuli the potential president became a lonely, depressed man, victimized by a vicious regime that inflicted upon him a slow death by a thousand cuts.[126]

When the government stripped his chieftainship in 1952, Luthuli anticipated correctly that his political path might lead to "ridicule, imprisonment . . . banishment and even death," but he prayed to God that he would continue to have the courage to fight for "a true democracy and a true union . . . of all the communities in the land."[127] While in Oslo, Luthuli had refused to go into exile, vowing to "win or die" in South Africa.[128] On July 21, 1967, the chief died having fought the good fight. A South African Railways freight train struck him while he walked across a train bridge near his Groutville home, and he died at the hospital that afternoon before he could convey his version of this tragic event.[129] Was Luthuli's death a deliberate assassination or an unfortunate accident? The official inquest concluded that Luthuli died of a fractured skull, cerebral hemorrhage, and contusion of the brain, and found

The Reverend Nimrod Ngcobo and members of Luthuli's family at Luthuli's funeral, Groutville, 1967. (Luthuli Museum)

no one criminally liable, claiming instead that Luthuli's failing eyesight and supposedly poor hearing made him unable to see or hear the oncoming train.[130] Given that the apartheid regime routinely murdered, tortured, and jailed its political opponents, it is not surprising that family members, close friends, colleagues, and subsequent generations have doubted an inquest report generated by the state. Describing "the alleged accident" in a letter to Mary-Louise Hooper, Nokukhanya denied reports that Luthuli was "blind, deaf, crossing a line where there was no pedestrian track. This is *all* a lie."[131] While further investigation may yield more definitive answers, whether his tragic encounter with the train was by accident or by design, Luthuli died imprisoned by apartheid.

Coda

The ANC's obituary praised Luthuli as "one of Africa's greatest political figures of our times; the undisputed leader and respected spokesman for South Africa's 14 million oppressed, exploited and humiliated inhabitants."[1] African liberation movements and American and European solidarity movements eulogized Luthuli, as did US Representative Barratt O'Hara of Illinois in the United States Congress.[2] Diplomats from seven countries, including the United States and Britain, attended the funeral. An American television broadcast recorded the conspicuous presence of security police in front of Luthuli's Groutville church, and many of the ten thousand funeral attendees wore ANC uniforms and colors, waved ANC flags, and sang freedom songs at his funeral. Nkosinathi Yengwa, brother of Luthuli political confidante M. B. Yengwa, delivered Luthuli's *izibongo*. Reflecting Luthuli's high esteem, Yengwa took the unusual step of linking the commoner Luthuli with Zulu royalty, using King Shaka's most famous praise names to describe the deceased ANC president. Yengwa sang verses of Luthuli's songs rendered during the chief's presidential address at the 1953 ANC national conference, lamenting land dispossession: "We the black nation, mourn for our land, which was taken away by the whites, they must leave our land alone." Echoing Luthuli's old adversary George Champion, who eulogized Luthuli as the "gutsiest of all Africa's leaders," and noting that Luthuli had outlived his adversaries, successive National Party prime ministers Malan, Strijdom, and Verwoerd, Nkosinathi praised Luthuli's moral authority, integrity, and courage. Luthuli was truly the Chief of the People.[3]

Conversely, after Luthuli's death, South African Security Police chief Hendrik van den Bergh sought to exploit the chief's status as a global icon of peace. He claimed that Luthuli respected the government's "honesty of purpose" and had planned to renounce communism and ANC violence because he realized belatedly that the ANC was a communist front organization.[4] This was not the first time that the State had used these tactics. In May 1963, authorities fabricated a letter, allegedly written by Luthuli, which was posted to UN secretary-general U Thant. The forgery offered to "guide" the UN diplomat's Cold War–era "deliberations" and affirm the principle of nonviolence "touch[ing] the hearts of the South African government." It further condemned the extremism of exiled ANC socialists, disparaging them as "puppet politicians" who brainwash their underlings and "cause the Government to arm themselves to the teeth," delaying a negotiated solution.[5] Alerted to the fraud, Luthuli vehemently replied, "I would sooner see myself dead than be an author of such a letter."[6] Nokukhanya denounced van den Bergh's fraudulent attempts to advance apartheid propaganda, and the ANC journal *Sechaba* argued forcefully that Luthuli "did not falter" when the ANC "officially and constitutionally changed" its policy to sanction violence.[7] Luthuli's amanuensis Charles Hooper recalled that Luthuli "used the analogy of a person using violence to defend his family against an attack by a violent mad man."[8] "Publicly, [Luthuli] advocated only non-violence and dialogue because they were what he passionately wanted South Africans to believe in; but privately he maintained that Stauffenberg was right in trying to destroy Hitler.... [Luthuli's] condemnation of violence was conditional and qualified."[9]

Contrary to van den Bergh's claim, Luthuli was neither a victim of ANC fanatics bent on guerrilla warfare nor an unyielding opponent of military struggle. Despite the stirring campaigns of nonviolence and the revolutionary and inspirational visions of a harmonious, multiracial postapartheid South Africa that contributed to his Nobel Peace Prize, the apartheid regime and its increasingly supportive electorate offered no concessions. The late historian Stephen Ellis pointed to the December 1960 SACP conference as the decisive moment that MK "had its immediate origin in the Communist Party rather than in the ANC," who were "bounced" into "South Africa's armed struggle [that] was from the outset inscribed in the politics of the Cold War."[10] But since at least the early 1950s, some ANC leaders, including Mandela, had felt that some form of armed self-defense was inevitable.[11] The Sharpeville-Langa massacres and subsequent government repression provoked moves toward armed struggle by some leaders of the ANC, PAC, and SACP, among other groups. These leaders were mindful that late-1950s African rural and urban rebellions against Bantu Authorities reflected an increasingly militant mood. The historical trajectory of racial segregation and apartheid, supported since the beginning of the Cold War by powerful allies like the United States and Great Britain, seemed to foreclose any possibility of dialogue and peace.[12] In this high-stakes context, Luthuli and other Congress Alliance leaders authorized the separate formation of MK and its measures of self-defense and sabotage while insisting that the ANC would maintain its nonviolent policies. As an astute leader who had already faced the hydra-headed vengeance of the state, the president-general still hoped the ANC would maintain its foundational policies while MK fulfilled its mandate to destroy government property and avoid any bloodshed. Alas, it was not to be so.

The chief's death coincided with fundamental changes in the liberation struggle. As South Africa seemed to crush domestic resistance, its long-standing Cold War geopolitical alliances with Great Britain and America solidified around increasing trade and investment ties with a booming South African economy built on cheap black labor. Holding permanent seats on the UN Security Council, the United States and Great Britain vetoed antiapartheid resolutions that passed the General Assembly. Tambo lamented, "certainly for us the alternative to war disappeared when South Africa rejected the solution so ably and effectively advocated by the ANC under the leadership of the now late Chief Luthuli. With his death . . . the last hope for South Africa went."[13] Soon came MK's first military engagement with proapartheid military forces with the Tambo-named "Luthuli Detachment's" movement from Zambia into Southern Rhodesia in the Wankie and Sipolilo campaigns.[14]

The story of Albert Luthuli is at once one of untold tragedy and despair, prophetic triumph and a relevant model of leadership for today's South Africa. Though he would not live to see postapartheid South Africa, the president-general had prophesied, "South Africa will be free. I may not live to see that day, but my children will surely see it. . . . It is for us to devote ourselves to the task of human welfare, the cause of making liberty and happiness the possession of not only our own country but of all the oppressed people in the world."[15] On February 25, 1990, two weeks after his liberty was restored, Nelson Mandela addressed a mass rally in Durban, hoping to stem the rising tide of violence between ANC supporters and the rival Inkatha Freedom Party. Speaking of a united South Africa, Mandela invoked Luthuli's prophetic words: "I personally believe that here in South Africa, with all our diversities of color and race, we will show the world a new pattern for democracy. I think that there is a challenge to us in South Africa, to set a new example for the world." Imploring the crowd to heed Luthuli's vision, Mandela declared, "this is the challenge we face today."[16] Nokukhanya greeted Mandela at this rally before telling the crowd, "my wish before I die is to see blacks and whites living harmoniously in a united South Africa"—a dream deferred for her husband but one made possible for her to see with the establishment of a nonracial, democratic South Africa in 1994.[17]

It remains somewhat ironic—human history is like this—that though the image of the early 1990s Mandela resembled that of Luthuli thirty years earlier, the Mandela of the early 1960s led transformations within the ANC that eclipsed Luthuli's domestic leadership, even as he reached the apex of his global renown. As leader of MK, Mandela led the successful effort to have the ANC adopt armed struggle as a legitimate method in the antiapartheid movement, despite the deep reservations of Luthuli, who was a principled advocate of nonviolence. After he had initiated the transition to armed struggle thirty years earlier and thus become the de facto head of the ANC, and had served twenty-seven years in prison for his role in the sabotage campaigns against the apartheid regime, it was thus a considerable historical irony that the Mandela who emerged from prison often used the reconciliatory political language of his mentor, and sometimes rival, Albert Luthuli. Mandela followed Luthuli's leadership model of allying the courage, will, and vision to end oppression with the necessary understanding that peaceful resolution was better than vengeful violence in delivering a peaceful, nonracial, democratic postapartheid state. But now, long after Luthuli and Mandela have passed from the political scene, replaced by increasingly corrupt, self-serving leaders, we are reminded that quality leadership matters deeply. Luthuli's integrity, his gospel of service to the dispossessed, his collaborative leadership style, and his willingness to suffer and even die to realize a nonracial, democratic, and equitable South Africa are values deeply needed in today's South Africa, so that the post-1994 "born-free" generation of young people, many of whom are disillusioned and angered by the slow pace of transformation, can yet enjoy the fruits of his revolutionary vision.

Notes

Introduction: Who Was Albert Luthuli?

1. This biography is the first to make use of previously unavailable Luthuli papers at the Schomburg Center for Research in Black Culture, New York Public Library. I would like to thank Thandi Luthuli-Gcabashe, daughter of Albert and Nokukhanya Luthuli, who granted me permission to view these papers. I am also indebted to Robert R. Edgar for bringing these papers to my attention and to the Schomburg archivists, particularly Diana Lachatanere and Stephen Fullwood III, for facilitating access to these papers.

2. The ANC itself has exhibited some historical amnesia regarding Luthuli, scarcely acknowledging the recent fiftieth anniversaries of Luthuli's Nobel Peace Prize (2011) and Luthuli's death (2017).

3. Thula Simpson, *Umkhonto we Sizwe: The ANC's Armed Struggle* (Cape Town: Penguin Random House, 2016), 37–38.

Chapter One: The Education of a Zulu Christian

1. Albert Luthuli, *Let My People Go* (New York: McGraw-Hill, 1962), 24; Scott Couper, *Albert Luthuli: Bound by Faith* (Scottsville: University of Kwa-Zulu-Natal Press, 2010), 21.

2. Benedict Carton, "Awaken Nkunkulu, Zulu God of the Old Testament: Pioneering Missionaries during the Early Age of Racial Spectacle," in *Zulu Identities: Being Zulu, Past and Present*, ed. Benedict Carton, John Laband, and

Jabulani Sithole (Pietermaritzburg: University of KwaZulu-Natal Press, 2008), 133; Luthuli, *Let My People*, 19–22; Thomas J. Karis and Gail M. Gerhart, *Challenge and Violence, 1953–1964*, vol. 3 of *From Protest to Challenge: A Documentary History of African Politics in South Africa, 1882–1964*, ed. Thomas J. Karis and Gwendolen M. Carter (Stanford: Hoover Institution Press, 1977), 62–63.

3. Harvey Feinberg, *Our Land, Our Life, Our Future: Black South African Challenges to Territorial Segregation, 1913–1948* (Pretoria: UNISA Press, 2015).

4. Luthuli, *Let My People*, 26.

5. Ben Carton and Rob Morrell, "Competitive Combat, Warrior Bodies, and Zulu Sport: The Gender Relations of Stick Fighting in South Africa, 1800–1930," in *Beyond C. L. R. James: Shifting Boundaries of Race and Ethnicity in Sport*, ed. John Nauright, Alan Cobley, and David Wiggins (Fayetteville: University of Arkansas Press, 2014), 135–38, 140–41.

6. Luthuli, *Let My People*, 17.

7. Ibid., 29–30.

8. Couper, *Bound by Faith*, 29–30.

9. *Drum,* December 1961.

10. *Iso Lomuzi,* May 1933, December 1935.

11. David Anthony, *Max Yergan: Race Man, Internationalist, Cold Warrior* (New York: New York University Press, 2006), 66.

12. Peter Alegi, "Sport, Race, and Liberation: A Preliminary Study of Albert Luthuli's Sporting Life," in *Sport and Liberation in South Africa: Reflections and Suggestions*, ed. Cornelius Thomas (Alice: University of Fort Hare Press, 2006), 66–82.

13. Peter Rule, Marilyn Aitken, and Jenny Van Dyk, *Nokukhanya: Mother of Light* (Berkeley: University of California Press, 1993), 41, 57.

14. Ibid., 58.

15. Albertina Luthuli, "UBaba: Recollections by Ntombazana," in Albert Luthuli, *Luthuli: Speeches of Chief Albert Luthuli, 1898–1967*, comp. E. S. Reddy (Durban: Madiba, 1991), 13, 38.

1. I thank Jon Soske for this point. See Jon Soske, "How to Approach Heaven," *Chimurenga Chronic,* April 5, 2016, http://chimurengachronic.co.za/how-to-approach-heaven-2/.

2. Albert Luthuli, *Let My People Go* (New York: McGraw-Hill, 1962), 75; Logan Naidoo, *In the Shadow of Chief Luthuli: Reflections of Goolam Suleiman* (Groutville: Luthuli Museum, 2010), 12; Luthuli, letter to the editor, *Natal Mercury,* June 22, 1956.

3. G. Carter, interview with Chief Albert Luthuli, Durban, March 28, 1964, 1–2, C1, folder C, LP, Historical Papers Research Archive, Cullen Library Collection, University of Witwatersrand; Luthuli, *Let My People,* 22.

4. Luthuli, *Let My People,* 56–57, 61–62; Naidoo, *In the Shadow,* 15.

5. Peter Rule, Marilyn Aitken, and Jenny Van Dyk, *Nokukhanya: Mother of Light* (Berkeley: University of California Press, 1993), 92–93.

6. Luthuli, *Let My People,* 120.

7. *Drum,* December 1961.

8. Albert Luthuli, *Luthuli: Speeches of Chief Albert Luthuli, 1898–1967,* comp. E. S. Reddy (Durban: Madiba, 1991), 37; *Advance,* February 18, 1952; *Drum,* December 1961. Naidoo, *In the Shadow,*14.

9. *Johannesburg Sunday Times,* May 2, 1959.

10. Luthuli, *Let My People,* 76.

11. "Africans' Claims in South Africa," in Thomas J. Karis, *Hope and Challenge, 1935–152,* vol. 2 of *From Protest to Challenge: A Documentary History of African Politics in South Africa, 1882–1964,* ed. Thomas J. Karis and Gwendolen M. Carter (Stanford: Hoover Institution, 1973), 209–24.

12. NRC Meeting Minutes, box 1, folder 69, Albert Luthuli Papers, Schomburg Center (hereafter LPSC).

13. Albert Luthuli, "Fifty Years of Union—Political Review," December 21, 1959, box 4, folder 86, LPSC.

14. E. S. Reddy, "Gandhi and Africans in South Africa," box 1, folders 7, 33 in MS 1499, E. S. Reddy Papers, Yale University Library (hereafter ESRP).

15. David Chidester, *Religions of South Africa* (London: Routledge, 1992), 197.

16. Hermann Giliomee, *The Afrikaners: A Biography of a People* (Charlottesville: University of Virginia Press, 2009), 487.

17. Wilson Minton to Albert Luthuli, October 27, 1960, box 4, folder 73, LPSC.

18. Luthuli, *Let My People*, 81. Luthuli did not meet Mahatma Gandhi on this trip; personal communication with E. S. Reddy, September 15, 2015.

19. *Philadelphia Tribune*, January 18, 1949; *New Journal and Guide*, January 22, 1949; Albert Luthuli to Frederick Rowe, February 20, 1949, box 48, file 15, Phelps Stokes Papers, Schomburg Center (hereafter PSSC); *Cleveland Call and Post*, September 25, 1948.

20. Albert Luthuli, "Mahatma Gandhi Memorial Lecture," 3–4. Luthuli Museum, Groutville, South Africa.

21. Samuel Gandy to L. H. Foster, January 14, 1949, box 48, file 15, PSSC; *New Journal and Guide*, August 5, 1967; *Philadelphia Tribune*, January 18, 1949; *New Journal and Guide*, January 22, 1949.

22. Luthuli, *Let My People*, 83.

23. Ibid., 85; *New Journal and Guide*, August 5, 1967.

24. Nadine Gordimer, *Telling Times: Writing and Living, 1954–2008* (New York: W. W. Norton, 2010), 55.

25. Albert Luthuli, presidential address to the Natal Annual Provincial Conference, July 26, 1956, box 4, folder 19, LPSC; Robert Edgar and Myra Ann Houser, "'The Most Patient of Animals, Next to the Ass': Jan Smuts, Howard University, and African American Leadership, 1930," *Safundi* 18, no. 1 (2017): 29–51.

26. Albert Luthuli to Frederick Rowe, February 20, 1949, box 48, file 15, PSSC; Luthuli, *Let My People*, 86–90.

27. Steven Gish, *Alfred B. Xuma: African, American, South African* (New York: NYU Press, 2000), 160–61; *Fighting Talk*, November 1961.

28. George Champion to C. E. Ramohanoe, May 16, 1947, and George Champion to Msimang, July 22, 1947, box 6, folder 77, LPSC; George Champion to Selby Msimang, January 28, 1950, box 6, folder 69, LPSC.

29. Editorial, *Inkundla ya Bantu*, March 24, 1951, 3, in box 6, folder 99, LPSC.

30. Yengwa, quoted in Julie Frederikse, *The Unbreakable Thread: Non-racialism in South Africa* (Bloomington: Indiana University Press, 1990), 52; Karis, *Hope and Challenge*, 514; M. B. Yengwa, interview, November 1973, in London, England, box 6, folder 112, LPSC.

31. Gerald J. Pillay, *Voices of Liberation: Albert Luthuli* (Pretoria: HSRC Press, 1993), vii; *Ilanga Lase Natal*, June 4, 1951, box 6, folder 96, LPSC; George Champion to Albert Luthuli, September 1, 1951, box 6, folder 97, LPSC; George Champion to J. N. Nhlapo, June 3, 1953, box 6, folder 100, LPSC.

Chapter Three: The Nonviolent, Multiracial Politics of Defiance

1. Gerald J. Pillay, *Voices of Liberation: Albert Luthuli* (Pretoria: HSRC Press, 1993), 31.

2. *Indian Opinion*, February 20, 1953.

3. Mary Benson, *Chief Albert Lutuli of South Africa* (London: Oxford University Press, 1963), 19.

4. David Welsh, *The Rise and Fall of Apartheid* (Charlottesville: University of Virginia Press, 2009), 110–12; Minutes of the Meetings of the Working Committee of the African National Congress (Natal) Held on Saturday, September 10, 1952, at Lakhani Chambers, Saville Street, Durban, Luthuli Papers, Northwestern University (hereafter LPNU); Albert Luthuli pronouncement, "We Go to Action," August 30, 1952, LPNU.

5. Albert Luthuli, *Let My People Go* (New York: McGraw-Hill, 1962), 116.

6. *Indian Opinion*, January 21, 1949; Uma Mesthrie, *Gandhi's Prisoner? The Life of Gandhi's Son Manilal* (Cape Town: Kwela Books, 2004).

7. *Indian Opinion*, February 6, 20, 1953.

8. Kader Asmal, *Politics in My Blood: A Memoir* (Johannesburg: Jacana Press, 2011), 4.

9. Dorothy Nyembe, interview, in Julie Frederikse, *The Unbreakable Thread: Non-racialism in South Africa* (Bloomington: Indiana University Press, 1990), 54; Benson, *Chief Albert*

Lutuli, 19; Raymond Suttner and Jeremy Cronin, eds., *50 Years of the Freedom Charter* (Pretoria: UNISA Press, 2006), 46.

10. Scott Couper, "When Chief Albert Luthuli Launched 'Into the Deep': A Theological Reflection on a Homiletic Resource of Political Significance," *Journal of Theology for Southern Africa* 130 (March 2008): 82; Albert Luthuli, public statement, "The Road to Freedom is Via the Cross," November 15, 1952, reprinted in Albert Luthuli, *Luthuli: Speeches of Chief Albert Luthuli, 1898–1967*, comp. E. S. Reddy (Durban: Madiba, 1991), 10–13. The government dismissed Luthuli from the chieftainship on November 11, 1952.

11. Luthuli, "The Road to Freedom Is Via the Cross," 11.

12. Luthuli, *Let My People*, 147–48.

13. Deriving from the Dutch Reformed Church in the Netherlands, the largest denomination within South Africa's Dutch Reformed religious tradition is the Dutch Reformed Church (NGK), which began in what became South Africa in the seventeenth century. In the 1850s, there were two breakaway denominations, one known as the Dutch Reformed Church (NHK) and the other as the Reformed Churches of South Africa (GK). These three branches are all part of the Dutch Reformed Church tradition.

14. Richard Elphick, *The Equality of Believers: Protestant Missionaries and the Racial Politics of South Africa* (Charlottesville: University of Virginia Press, 2012), 250.

15. Ibid., 254, 255, 257.

16. Albert Luthuli, "Resist Apartheid" speech reprinted in Gerald Pillay, *Voices of Liberation: Albert Luthuli* (Pretoria: HSRC Press, 2012), 73.

17. Nelson Mandela, *Long Walk to Freedom* (Boston: Little Brown, 1994), 137–38; L. Kanyile to Luthuli, November 22, 1952, box 3, folder 92, LPSC); Walter Sisulu Memoir, MSS 294, 84, Robben Island Document (Walter Sisulu), box 1, folder 39, George Houser Papers, Michigan State University (hereafter Sisulu Robben Island Memoir); Bernard Magubane et al., *The Road to Democracy in South Africa*, vol. 1, *1960–1970* (Pretoria: UNISA Press, 2005).

18. Tom Lodge, *Mandela: A Critical Life* (New York: Oxford University Press, 2006), 54–55; *Spark*, January 30, 1953; Nelson Mandela, "No Easy Walk to Freedom," Transvaal ANC Presidential Address, September 21, 1953, in Thomas J. Karis and Gail M. Gerhart, *Challenge and Violence, 1953–1964*, vol. 3 of *From Protest to Challenge: A Documentary History of African Politics in South Africa, 1882–1964*, ed. Thomas J. Karis and Gwendolen M. Carter (Stanford: Hoover Institution Press, 1977), 109; *South Africa Freedom News*, August 21, 1963–June 30, 1965 folder, E. S. Reddy Papers, Yale University Library (hereafter ESRP).

19. Naidoo, *In the Shadow*, 20–21; Albertina Luthuli, "UBaba," in Luthuli, *Speeches*; Peter Rule, Marilyn Aitken, and Jenny Van Dyk, *Nokukhanya: Mother of Light* (Berkeley: University of California Press, 1993), 108.

20. *Bantu World*, May 22, 1953.

21. *Indian Opinion*, February 20, 27, 1953.

22. Albert Luthuli, "Our Vision Is A Democratic Society," in Pillay, *Voices of Liberation*, 116.

23. Jon Soske, *Internal Frontiers: African Nationalism and the Indian Diaspora in Twentieth-Century South Africa* (Athens: Ohio University Press, 2017).

24. *Indian Opinion*, February 6, 1953.

25. *Indian Opinion*, February 20, 1953.

26. Albert Luthuli and G. M. Naicker, "Message to Those Staying at Home April 14, 15th and 16th," 1953(?), LPNU.

27. Albert Luthuli, "An Urgent Call / Dr. Naicker Pledges," June 1953, Historical Papers Research Archive, Cullen Library Collection, University of Witwatersrand (hereafter WITS), AD 2186, file Fa 21.

28. "An Urgent Call by Chief A. J. Luthuli," June 1953, LPNU; Mary-Louise Hooper, June 26, 1959, Memoirs SA folder, Mary-Louise Hooper Papers, Special Collections, Michigan State University (hereafter MLHP).

29. *Bantu World*, June 6, 1953. Luthuli's colleagues G. M. Naicker, SAIC president, and M. B. Yengwa, Natal ANC secretary, faced the same ban. See *Indian Opinion*, June 5, 1953.

House of Assembly Debates, 1953, column 202, in Henry Kenney, *Architect of Apartheid: H. F. Verwoerd—An Appraisal* (Johannesburg: Jonathan Ball, 1980), 136.

30. *Baltimore Afro-American,* June 27, 1953.

31. Recorded conversation between South African Brigadier-General Rademeyer and an unidentified Basutoland security officer, July 17, 1954, at police headquarters (unidentified city). DO (Dominion Office) 119/1180 Intelligence Organisations in High Commission Territories, 1953–55, National Archives, UK.

32. Couper, "Launched 'Into the Deep.'"

33. Leslie Bank and Benedict Carton, "Forgetting Apartheid: History, Culture and the Body of a Nun," *Africa* 86, no. 3 (2016): 473; Luthuli, *Let My People*, 127.

34. Mandela, *Long Walk*, 136; Nelson Mandela, *Conversations with Myself* (New York: Picador Press, 2011), 115; Robert R. Edgar and Luyanda ka Msumza, eds., *Africa's Cause Must Triumph: The Collected Writings of A. P. Mda* (Johannesburg: HSRC Press, 2018); Oliver Tambo, interview, November 15, 1963, in Luli Callinicos, *Oliver Tambo: Beyond the Engeli Mountains* (Cape Town: David Philip, 2004), 281.

35. Bernard Magubane, Philip Bonner, Jabulani Sithole, Peter Delius, Janet Cherry, Pat Gibbs, and Thozama April, "The Turn to Armed Struggle," in Magubane et al., *The Road to Democracy*, 1:60.

36. Sisulu Robben Island Memoir.

37. Albert Luthuli to Walter Sisulu, June 22, 1953; statement, Chief Albert J. Luthuli, 1956, 13, R. v. Adams and others, folder B8–10, LP, WITS.

38. *Daily Dispatch,* February 14, 1953.

39. Albert Luthuli to Z. K. Matthews, June 15, 1953, folder A1, LP, WITS. I am grateful to Benedict Carton for this source.

40. *Indian Opinion,* January 2, 1953; January 23, 1953; and January 30, 1953.

41. *Drum,* January 1955; Jordan Ngubane, *An African Explains Apartheid* (New York: Praeger Books, 1963), 163–67.

42. *Drum,* January 1955.

43. D. Steere, "Albert Luthuli: Head of the African National Congress," Luthuli file (1), box 37, folder 29, American Board of Commissioners of Foreign Missions Papers, Houghton Library, Harvard University. Steere compiled this document shortly "after autumn 1952."

44. Elinor Sisulu, *Walter and Albertina Sisulu: In Our Lifetime* (Cape Town: Abacus Books, 2003), 183.

45. Mandela, *Long Walk*, 137; Mandela, *Conversations*, 115.

46. Peter Delius, interview with John Nkadimeng and J. Phala, June 17, 1993, Wits History Workshop; Magubane et al., "The Turn to Armed Struggle," 57–58.

47. William Duiker, *Ho Chi Minh: A Life* (New York: Hyperion, 2000), 455; Magubane et al., "The Turn to Armed Struggle," 55.

48. Elphick, *The Equality of Believers*, 288.

49. "1953 Natal Provincial Presidential Address," October 31, 1953, Documents Concerning Chief Lutuli, 1953–1962, ESRP.

50. Naidoo, *In the Shadow*, 22–23.

51. Luthuli, *Let My People*, 47–49.

52. Pillay, *Voices of Liberation*, 77.

53. Oliver Tambo to ANC Provincial Secretaries, April 19, 1955, box 3, folder 32, LPSC; Joe Matthews to Albert Luthuli, May 2, 1955, box 3, folder 33, LPSC; Report of the Provincial Executive for the Year Commencing November 1, 1954, and Ending September 30, 1955, LPNU; Minutes of the Meeting of the Provincial Committee of the ANC, January 21–22, 1955, LPNU; *Indian Opinion*, March 25, 1955.

54. *Bantu World*, April 23, 1955; "United Nations Commission on the Racial Situation in the Union of South Africa," Part II, South Africa 1966–68 folder, ESRP.

55. Gail M. Gerhart, *Black Power: The Evolution of an Ideology* (Berkeley: University of California Press, 1978), 129–72.

56. G. Carter, interview with Chief Albert Luthuli, Durban, March 28, 1964, 1–2, C1, folder C, LP, WITS; Luthuli's message, "Annual Report of N.E.C. to A.N.C., 16th to 19th December 1954," Preparatory Examination in the Magistrate's Court for the District of Johannesburg, 23, December 19, 1956,

Regina versus Farrid Adams and Others, 1956 Treason Trial, A1.b1, vol.1, box 2, AD 1812, WITS.

57. Albert Luthuli, presidential address, ANC Annual Conference, December 16–19, 1954, in Karis and Gerhart, *Challenge and Violence*, 135–41.

58. Ben Turok, *Nothing but the Truth: Behind the ANC's Struggle Politics* (Johannesburg: Jonathan Ball, 2003), 67, Natal Action Committee Congress of the People, September 6, 1954, box 3, folder 7, LPSC.

59. Lionel Bernstein, *Memory against Forgetting: Memoirs from a Life in South African Politics, 1938–1964* (London: Viking Press, 1999), 145.

60. Ibid., 42; "Notes from Z. K. Matthews," box 4, folder 11, LPSC.

61. Albert Luthuli, message to the Congress of the People meeting, June 25, 1955, box 4, folder 86, LPSC; Pillay, *Voices of Liberation*, 75.

62. *Fighting Talk*, October 1954, box 6, folder 115, LPSC; "Legal Struggle to Resist Apartheid and for Charter," *New Age*, November 25, 1954, in Documents concerning Chief Lutuli, Photocopies, 1953–1962, ESRP; Albert Luthuli, presidential message to Natal ANC Annual Conference, October 30, 1954, box 3, folder 11, LPSC.

63. Suttner and Cronin, *Freedom Charter*, 46.

64. Albertina Sisulu, interview, "Road to Resistance, 1948–1964," in Connie Field, *Have You Heard from Johannesburg: Seven Stories from the Global Anti-apartheid Movement* (Berkeley, CA: Clarity Films, 2010).

65. Martin Meredith, *Mandela: A Biography* (New York: Public Affairs Books, 2011), 135; Scott Couper, *Albert Luthuli: Bound by Faith* (Scottsville: University of Kwa-Zulu-Natal Press, 2010), 68; Sisulu Robben Island Memoir, 106; Rule, Aitken, and Van Dyk, *Nokukhanya*, 109–10.

66. Albert Luthuli and M. B. Yengwa, "Joint Message to the Congress of the People of South Africa: Meeting in Kliptown, Johannesburg," June 25–26, 1955, box 3, folder 54, LPSC.

67. "Congress of the People: Kliptown, Johannesburg," June 25 and 26, 1955, box 3, folder 63, LPSC.

68. Suttner and Cronin, *Freedom Charter*, 100.

69. Luthuli, *Let My People,* 142.

70. Albert Luthuli, presidential address to Provincial Natal ANC annual meeting, July 26, 1956, box 4, folder 19, LPSC; Albert Luthuli to Mary-Louise Hooper, June 8, 1956, box 4, folder 1, LPSC; Luthuli, presidential address, July 26, 1956, box 3, folder 87, LPSC; Suttner and Cronin, *Freedom Charter,* 115; *New Age,* August 2, 1956.

71. Report of the National Executive Committee of the African National Congress, December 17–18, 1955, in Karis and Gerhart, *Challenge and Violence,* 3, 223–24.

72. Jon Soske, "'Wash Me Black Again': African Nationalism, the Indian Diaspora, and Kwa-Zulu Natal, 1944–1960" (PhD diss., University of Toronto, 2009), 247; Albert Luthuli to Archie Gumede, September 5, 1955, box 3, folder 84, LPSC.

73. Albert Luthuli to Mary-Louise Hooper, June 8, 1956, box 4, folder 1, LPSC; Report of the 46th ANC Annual National Conference, December 13–14, 1958, box 4, folder 32, LPSC.

74. *World,* January 28, 1956; Arthur Letele to Albert Luthuli, April 22, 1956, box 3, folder 105, LPSC; Albert Luthuli to Mary-Louise Hooper, June 8, 1956, box 4, folder 1, LPSC; Gerhart, *Black Power.*

75. Chief Langallake Ngcobo, A. W. G. Champion, and H. Selby Msimang to "PA," April 18, 1956, box 3, folder 97, LPSC; Albert Luthuli to unknown recipient, May 22, 1956, ANC papers, WITS.

76. *Drum,* December 1, 1955.

77. *Drum,* February 1956.

78. *Liberation,* April 18, 1956, in *South Africa's Radical Tradition: A Documentary History,* ed. Allison Drew, vol. 2, *1943–1964* (Cape Town: Buchu Books, 1997), 104.

79. *New Age,* February 23, 1956, in Documents concerning Chief Lutuli, Photocopies, 1953–1962, ESRP.

80. Albert Luthuli to Dr. Dadoo, September 2, 1955, folder A1, LP, WITS. I am grateful to Ben Carton for this reference.

81. Natal ANC 1955 Annual Provincial Conference Resolutions, October 8–10, 1955, box 3, folder 82, LPSC; Albert Luthuli to Oliver Tambo, March 19, 1956, box 3, folder 91, LPSC; Albert Luthuli to Z. K. Matthews, March 22, 1956, box 3, folder

91, LPSC; Albert Luthuli to Arthur Letele, March 22, 1956, box 3, folder 91, LPSC.

82. Treason Trial transcript AD 1812, vol. 57/11575, in David Everatt, *The Origins of Non-racialism* (Johannesburg: University of Witwatersrand Press, 2010), 105.

83. Memorandum of Anti-Pass Campaign, issued by the National Consultative Committee, November 10, 1956, LPNU.

84. Naidoo, *In the Shadow*, chap. 1.

85. Ibid., 24–25; Mary-Louise Hooper, "In the Rain with Zami," MLHP.

86. Minutes of the Meeting of the Provincial Committee of the ANC, Natal Branch, January 21–22, 1955, in box 3, folder 51, LPSC; Albert Luthuli to "Dear Friend," June 8, 1956, box 4, folder 1, LPSC; Luthuli, *Let My People*, 193.

87. *New Age*, August 2, 1956, Documents concerning Chief Luthuli folder, ESRP.

88. Minutes, Provincial Executive ANC Natal, Nov. 26–27, 1955; Albert Luthuli to Mary-Louise Hooper, July 2, 1956, LPNU; Minutes of the Meeting of the Provincial Executive Committee of the ANC, January 21–22, 1956, box 4, folder 16, LPSC.

89. Organizational Report of Florence Mkhize, LPNU.

90. Memorandum of Anti-Pass Campaign, Issued by the National Consultative Committee, November 10, 1956, LPNU.

91. Dorothy Nyembe, interview, in Frederikse, *The Unbreakable Thread*, 54.

92. Albert Luthuli to Mary-Louise Hooper, June 8, 1956, box 4, folder 1, LPSC; George Houser, *No One Can Stop the Rain* (Cleveland: Pilgrim Press, 1989)

93. See Albert Luthuli to Mary-Louise Hooper, August 2, 1955, Luthuli letters file, MLHP; Mary-Louise Hooper, "Birthday," Memoirs folder, Hooper to Luthuli ("Abou Jaffer"), October 22, 1960, MLHP; Albert Luthuli to Senator L. Rubin, May 24, 1956, box 3, folder 91, LPSC; Ismail Meer, *A Fortunate Man* (Cape Town: Struik, 2002), 191–92.

94. Mary-Louise Hooper, "Night Drive in the Rain with Zami—1956," Memoirs folder, MLHP.

95. Callinicos, *Oliver Tambo*, 193; Couper, *Bound by Faith*, 66; Soske, "'Wash Me Black Again,'" 185.

96. Mary-Louise Hooper, undated notes, "Reflections of Chief," MLHP.

97. Albertina Luthuli, interview, in Luthuli, *Speeches*, 29.

98. Albert Luthuli, letter of introduction for Mary-Louise Hooper, July 2, 1956, box 3, folder 91, LPSC; ANC, letter of introduction for Mary-Louise Hooper, n.d., box 4, folder 1, LPSC; Mary-Louise Hooper to Albert Luthuli, February 7, 1960, Hooper to Luthuli, October 22, 1960, and Mary-Louise Hooper to Ruth First, n but ca.d.. 1962, About and to Chief, Nok, Albertinah, etc. folder, MLHP; Chief Lutuli and the United Nations folder, p. 3, ESRP.

99. Albert Luthuli to Arthur Letele, March 22, 1956, box 3, folder 91, LPSC; Albert Luthuli to George Houser, October 15, 1956, Chief Luthuli letters folder, MLHP 95.

100. Albert Luthuli to Mary-Louise Hooper, June 8, 1956, box 4, folder 1, LPSC. Rowley Arenstein was the honorary legal advisor to Congress. Minutes of the Meetings of the Working Committee of the African National Congress (Natal) Held on Saturday, September 10, 1952, at Lakhani Chambers, Saville Street, Durban, LPNU.

101. Anthony Sampson, *Mandela* (London: HarperCollins, 2011), 103; Albert Luthuli to Mary-Louise Hooper, June 8, 1956, folder 1, box 4, LPSC; C. Williams to Albert Luthuli, May 25, 1956, folder 92, box 3, LPSC. Paul Robeson donated proceeds from a benefit concert in London: "Recent Fund-Raising," folder 38, box 4, LPSC.

102. Rule, Aitken, and Van Dyk, *Nokukhanya*, 112–13, Luthuli, *Speeches*, 29; Mary-Louise Hooper, "Profile—Albert John Luthuli of South Africa," Memoirs S.A. folder, MLHP.

103. Albert Luthuli to Mary-Louise Hooper, June 8, 1956, box 4, folder 1, LPSC.

104. Naidoo, *In the Shadow*, 35; Benson, *Chief Albert Lutuli*, 30.

105. Sampson, *Mandela*, 103; Luthuli, foreword to Helen Joseph, *If This Be Treason* (New York: Contra Mundum Press, 1998), 9.

106. Walter Sisulu, interview, in Magubane et al., *The Road to Democracy*, vol. 1, 65.

107. Raymond Suttner, *The ANC Underground in South Africa* (Johannesburg: Jacana Media, 2008), 47.

108. Turok, *Nothing But*, 76–77.

109. Pillay, *Voices of Liberation*, 17; Sisulu Robben Island Memoir.

110. Meredith, *Mandela*, 132; Callinicos, *Oliver Tambo*, 188.

111. Denis Herbstein, *White Lies: Canon Collins and the Secret War against Apartheid* (London: James Currey, 2004).

112. Mandela, *Conversations*, 76.

113. Lillian Ngoyi, Treason Trial Transcript, AD 1812 A1–B1, vol. 10, 1873, George Houser Papers, Michigan State University (hereafter HP), WITS.

114. Meredith, *Mandela*, 145.

115. Luthuli, *Speeches*, 55, 58–59; Report of the Provincial Executive for the Year Commencing November 1, 1954, and Ending September 30, 1955, LPNU.

116. Albert Luthuli to Johannes Strydom, May 28, 1957, box 4, folder 21, LPSC.

117. "The IDAMF Conference," December 3–5, 1957, box 4, folder 25, LPSC.

118. Albert Luthuli, presidential address, ANC annual conference, December 14–16, 1957, box 4, folder 30, LPSC.

119. Albert Luthuli, "From the African National Congress, c. early 1958," box 6, folder 115, LPSC; *New Age*, November 7, 1957.

120. Luthuli, *Let My People*, 9.

121. Benson, *Chief Albert Lutuli*, 37.

122. Naidoo, *In the Shadow*, 45.

123. "Freedom Is the Apex," 1959, LPNU; Sisulu Robben Island Memoir, 120.

124. *Liberation*, July 1959.

125. Ruth First to Mary-Louise Hooper, May 13, 1959, About and to Chief, Nok, Albertinah, etc. folder, MLHP; Sisulu Robben Island Memoir.

126. Ruth First to Mary-Louise Hooper, May 13, 1959, About and to Chief, Nok, Albertinah, etc. folder, MLHP; *Johannesburg Sunday Times*, May 2, 1959.

127. Benson, *Chief Albert Lutuli*, 2; F. W. De Klerk, *The Last Trek—A New Beginning* (New York: St. Martin's Press, 1998), 31.

128. *Christian Science Monitor*, June 15, 1959; Luthuli, *Let My People*, 212; C.O.D. press statement, "Attack on Chief Luthuli," n.d., box 4, folder 39, LPSC; Mary-Louise Hooper, account of Albert Luthuli, n.d., Memoirs S.A. folder, MLHP.

129. Rule, Aitken, and Van Dyk, *Nokukhanya*, 106.

130. Charles Hooper, "Chief Luthuli: "He Knows the Woes of Landless Squatters," *Fighting Talk* 16, no. 1 (February 1962).

131. Minister of Justice C. Swart to Albert Luthuli, May 22, 1959, folder 72, box 4, LPSC.

132. *Natal Daily News*, May 29, 1959; *Natal Mercury*, May 28, 1959; *Natal Daily News*, June 1, 1959.

133. *Natal Daily News*, May 29, 1959.

134. *Sunday Times*, May 31, 1959; *Natal Daily News*, May 28, 1959; *Sunday Tribune*, May 31, 1959; *Sunday Express*, May 31, 1959.

135. *Natal Daily News*, May 31, 1959; *Natal Mercury*, May 31, 1959.

136. *Liberation*, July 1959.

137. Albert Luthuli, address to the Annual Conference of the ANCYL, July 8, 1959, box 4, folder 69, LPSC.

138. Pillay, *Voices of Liberation*, 27; Couper, *Bound by Faith*, 83.

139. Luthuli, *Let My People*, 218.

140. Ibid., 219; Pillay, *Voices of Liberation*, 23.

141. *Liberation*, February 23, 1957. "Sisulu Material from Karis," MSS 294, box 5, folder 83, HP; Magubane et al., *The Road to Democracy*, vol. 3, *International Solidarity*, pt. 1 (Pretoria: UNISA Press, 2008), 22–23 ; *Sechaba* (August 1984), 13; Mary Benson, *A Far Cry: The Making of a South African* (London: Penguin Books, 1990), 146.

142. Pillay, *Voices of Liberation*, 24.

143. Sifiso Ndlovu, "The ANC and the World, 1960–1970," in Magubane et al., *The Road to Democracy*, 1:549–50.

144. Asmal, *Politics in My Blood*, 6.

145. Peter Limb, "The Anti-Apartheid Movements in Australia and Aotearoa / New Zealand," in Magubane et al., *The Road to Democracy*, vol. 3, pt. 2, 910.

146. William Minter and Sylvia Hill, "Anti-Apartheid Solidarity in United States–South Africa Relations: From the Margins to the Mainstream," in Magubane et al., *The Road to Democracy*, vol. 3, pt. 2, 767.

147. *Sunday Times*, September 20, 1959; *New Age*, December 3, 1959.

148. Albert Luthuli, "Fifty Years of Union—Political Review," box 4, folder 86, LPSC.

149. *Drum*, June 1958.

150. Oliver Tambo, Report of the National Executive to the Transvaal Special Conference, November 1, 1958, box 4, folder 31, LPSC.

151. Report of the 46th ANC Annual National Conference, December 13–14, 1958, box 4, folder 32, LPSC.

152. *Our Africa*, January 1961.

153. *Drum*, November 1959; Arianna Lissoni, "Transformations in the ANC External Mission and Umkhonto we Sizwe, c. 1960–1969," *Journal of Southern African Studies* 35, no. 2 (2009): 292.

154. Albert Luthuli, speech, Durban, April 15, 1958, box 4, folder 79, LPSC.

155. "Notes for Delegates to the All African People's Conference to Be Held in Accra, Ghana in December 1958," box 4, folder 32, LPSC.

156. Albert Luthuli, presidential address, December 11, 1958, box 6, folder 115, LPSC.

157. *Christian Science Monitor*, June 15, 1959; *Liberation*, July 1959.

Chapter Four: Apartheid Violence and Armed Self-Defense

1. Hendrik Verwoerd, *Verwoerd Speaks: Speeches, 1948–1966*, ed. A. N. Pelzer (Johannesburg: APB, 1966), 23–29.

2. Hendrik Verwoerd, quoted in Connie Field, *The Road to Resistance*, pt. 1 of *Have You Heard from Johannesburg: Seven Stories from the Global Anti-apartheid Movement* (Berkeley, CA: Clarity Films, 2010).

3. Albert Luthuli, *Let My People Go* (New York: McGraw-Hill, 1962), 203.

4. Albert Luthuli, address to Conference on the Group Areas Act Convened by the Natal Indian Congress, May 5–6, 1956, box 3, folder 96, LPSC.

5. Gerald J. Pillay, *Voices of Liberation: Albert Luthuli* (Pretoria: HSRC Press, 1993), 111–12; Albert Luthuli, "Fifty Years of Union—Political Review," box 4, folder 86, LPSC; *Wall Street Journal*, January 11, 1960.

6. "Freedom Calendar," box 5, folder 23, LPSC; *Counter Attack*, October 1959.

7. Peter Delius, *Sebatakgomo, Migrant Organization, the ANC and the Sekhukuneland Revolt* (Johannesburg; University of Witwatersrand Press, 1990); Bernard Magubane, Philip Bonner, Jabulani Sithole, Peter Delius, Janet Cherry, Pat Gibbs, and Thozama April, "The Turn to Armed Struggle," in Bernard Magubane et al., *The Road to Democracy in South Africa*, vol. 1, *1960–1970* (Pretoria: UNISA Press, 2005), 58–59; interviews with D. Goldberg, R. Bernstein, H. Gwala, and B. Nair in Bernard Magubane et al., *The Road to Democracy in South Africa: South Africans Telling Their Stories, 1950–1970*, vol. 1 (Pretoria: UNISA Press, 2008), 339, 363–66.

8. SAPA Durban representative to Albert Luthuli, Aug 25, 1959, folder 71, box 4, LPSC; interview with Curnick Ndlovu in Magubane et al., "The Turn to Armed Struggle," 59; Justice "Gizenga" Mpanza, interview, in Magubane et al., *Telling Their Stories*, 339.

9. *Natal Mercury*, December 14, 1959.

10. *Star*, February 23, 1960; *Drum*, March 1960.

11. Philip Frankel, *An Ordinary Atrocity: Sharpeville and Its Massacre* (New Haven: Yale University Press, 2001), 53–180; Tom Lodge, *Sharpeville: An Apartheid Massacre and Its Consequences* (Oxford: Oxford University Press, 2011).

12. George Houser, testimony to the UN Special Committee on Apartheid, May 1963, folder 1963, ERP; Benjamin Pogrund, *Robert Sobukwe: How Can Man Die Better* (Johannesburg: Jonathan Ball Press, 2015).

13. Gail Gerhart, *Black Power: The Evolution of an Ideology* (Berkeley: University of California Press, 1978), 247.

14. Ahmed Kathrada, *No Bread for Mandela: Memoirs of Ahmed Kathrada, Prisoner No. 468/64* (Lexington: University of Kentucky Press, 2011), 127; Martin Meredith, *Mandela: A Biography* (New York: Public Affairs Books, 2011), 174; Luli Callinicos, *Oliver Tambo: Beyond the Engeli Mountains* (Cape Town: David Philip, 2004), 255; *Washington Post*, May 27, 1960.

15. *Commonwealth News*, December 19, 1960; *Natal Mercury*, October 22,1961.

16. Lodge, *Sharpeville*, 215–16.

17. Ben Turok, *Nothing but the Truth: Behind the ANC's Struggle Politics* (Johannesburg: Jonathan Ball, 2003).

18. Vladimir Shubin, *The ANC: A View from Moscow* (Johannesburg: Jacana Press, 2009), 26; Stephen Ellis, *External Mission: The ANC in Exile, 1960–1990* (Oxford: Oxford University Press, 2013), 12.

19. Ellis, *External Mission,* 17; Paul S. Landau, "Controlled by Communists? (Re)Assessing the ANC in Its Exilic Decades," *South African Historical Journal* 67, no. 2 (2015): 224; Bob Hepple, *Young Man with a Red Tie: A Memoir of Mandela and the Failed Revolution, 1960–1963* (Auckland Park: Jacana Media, 2013), 36, 104–106.

20. Thula Simpson, "Nelson Mandela and the Genesis of the ANC's Doomed Struggle: Notes on Method," *Journal of Southern African Studies* 44, no. 1 (2018): 133–78 and Paul Landou, "The ANC, MK, and 'The Turn to Violence' (1960–1962)," *South African Historical Journal* 64, no. 3 (2012): 538–63. There is evidence that by 1960 Mandela had joined the SACP Central Committee: Ellis, *External Mission,* 12–13; Landau, "Controlled by Communists?," 223–24, 240; Tom Lodge, "Secret Party: South African Communists between 1950 and 1960," *South African Historical Journal* 67, no. 4 (2015): 459–62.

21. Philip Bonner, "The Antinomies of Nelson Mandela," in *The Cambridge Companion to Nelson Mandela*, ed. Rita Barnard (New York: Cambridge University Press, 2014), 41; Turok, *Nothing But*, 123.

22. *New Age*, April 13, 1961; "The African Leaders Call to the African People of South Africa, Prepare for the All-In African Conference, March 1961," folder 115, box 6, LPSC.

23. Saul Dubow, *Apartheid, 1948–1994* (Oxford: Oxford University Press, 2014), 83–84; Herman Giliomee, *The Last Afrikaner Leaders: A Supreme Test of Power* (Charlottesville: University of Virginia Press, 2012), 74–77.

24. Bonner, "The Antimonies," 42; Nelson Mandela, *Long Walk to Freedom* (Boston: Little Brown, 1994), 236.

25. Callinicos, *Oliver Tambo*, 281.

26. Frantz Fanon, *Wretched of the Earth* (New York: Grove Press, 1963), 73.

27. Allison Drew, ed. *South Africa's Radical Tradition*, vol. 2, *1943–1964* (Cape Town: Buchu Books, 1997), 344.

28. Luthuli, *Let My People*, 113.

29. Ibid., 207.

30. The British Foreign Office called Luthuli's ANC "tailor-made for Communist exploitation": P. Liesching, High Commissioner in South Africa to Secretary of State for Commonwealth Relations, December 13, 1957, marked SECRET, 149 (53953), 29, Correspondence Respecting Commonwealth Relations, January–December 1957, vol. 3, DO 208, PRO. This finding echoed a secret CIA report, "Subversive Movements in South Africa," May 10, 1963, 2–3, CIA NLK-76–299, Digital National Security Archive, http://search.proquest.com.mutex.gmu.edu/dnsa/docview/ (accessed January 1, 2015).

31. Albert Luthuli to Z. K. Matthews, June 15, 1953, Folder A, "Intetho Esingisele Kuma Afrika Asekoloni," May 25, 1952, Exhibit HH, *Regina v. Njongwe*, LP Historical Papers Research Archive, Cullen Library Collection, University of Witwatersrand (hereafter WITS).

32. Mandela, *Long Walk*, 236.

33. Thula Simpson, *Umkhonto we Sizwe: The ANC's Armed Struggle* (Cape Town: Penguin Press 2016), 30–31.

34. Mandela, *Long Walk*, 236–37; David James Smith, *Young Mandela* (Boston: Little, Brown, 2010), 246–47.

35. Smith, *Young Mandela*, 238; Turok, *Nothing But*, 123; Naidoo, *In the Shadow*, 21; Fred Dube, interview, in Magubane et al., *Telling Their Stories*, 105.

36. Smith, *Young Mandela*, 238, 243.

37. *Rand Daily Mail*, August 1, 1967.

38. Goolam Suleiman, interview, 2001, quoted in Stephen Coan, "The Real Luthuli," *Witness*, March 24, 2011.

39. Mary Benson, *Chief Albert Lutuli of South Africa* (London: Oxford University Press, 1963), 65.

40. Drew, *South Africa's Radical Tradition*, 344; Andrew Mlangeni and Elias Motsoaledi, interviews, in Magubane et al., "The Turn to Armed Struggle," 83–84.

41. Kader Asmal, *Politics in My Blood: A Memoir* (Johannesburg: Jacana Press, 2011), 143; Hepple, *Young Man with a Red Tie*, 107.

42. Mandela, *Long Walk*, 237.

43. Unpublished autobiography of M. B. Yengwa (1976), 106, Masabalala Yengwa Papers, Luthuli Museum, Groutville.

44. Joe Matthews and Curnick Ndlovu, interviews, in Magubane et al., "The Turn to Armed Struggle," 88–89.

45. Mandela, *Long Walk*, 237–38; Turok, *Nothing But*, 127; Asmal, *Politics in My Blood*, 143.

46. Ismail Meer, *A Fortunate Man* (Cape Town: Struik, 2002), 223–24.

47. Ibid., 224.

48. Simpson, *Umkhonto*, 33.

49. Walter Sisulu Memoir, MSS 294, 84, Robben Island Document (Walter Sisulu), box 1, folder 39, George Houser Papers, Michigan State University (hereafter Sisulu Robben Island Memoir), 128.

50. Mandela, *Long Walk*, 238; Nelson Mandela, *Conversations with Myself* (New York: Picador Press, 2011), 78.

51. Simpson, *Umkhonto*, 33; Meer, *A Fortunate Man*, 224; Natoo Babenia, *Memoirs of a Saboteur* (Cape Town: Mayibuye Books, 1995), 53.

52. Simpson, *Umkhonto*, 33–34.

53. Turok, *Nothing But*, 135; Meer, *Fortunate Man*, 224.

54. Mandela, *Long Walk*, 238; Smith, *Young Mandela*, 248–49; Joe Matthews, interview, in Magubane et al., *Telling Their Stories*, 19; Mandela, *Conversations with Myself*, 78.

55. Asmal, *Politics in My Blood*, 143.

56. Mandela, *Long Walk*, 246.

57. Ibid.; Smith, *Young Mandela*, 249.

58. Landau, "Controlled by Communists?," 229–31.

59. Brian Bunting, *Moses Kotane, South African Revolutionary: A Political Biography* (London: Inkululeko Press, 1975), 268–69; Joe Slovo, *The Unfinished Autobiography of ANC Leader Joe Slovo* (Melbourne: Ocean Press, 2002), 150.

60. Fred Dube, interview, in Magubane et al., *Telling Their Stories*, 105.

61. Albert Luthuli, Nobel lecture, Oslo University, December 11, 1961, typescript, folder B4–7, Luthuli Papers, A3337, WITS; Jabulani Sithole, "Chief Albert Luthuli and Bantustan Politics," in *Zulu Identities: Being Zulu, Past and Present*, ed. Benedict Carton, John Laband, and Jabulani Sithole (New York: Oxford University Press, 2009), 331.

62. *Christian Science Monitor*, December 9, 1961.

63. M. Hooper, "Profile—Albert John Luthuli, c. 1961," Memoirs S.A. folder, Mary-Louise Hooper Papers, Special Collections, Michigan State University (hereafter MLHP); *Natal Mercury*, October 24, 1961.

64. Benson, *Chief Albert Lutuli*, 47; *Sunday Tribune*, October 29, 1961.

65. *Sunday Tribune*, October 29, 1961; *Sunday Tribune*, November 5, 1961.

66. *Natal Mercury*, October 24, 1961; *Natal Daily News*, October 27, 1961.

67. Naidoo, *In the Shadow*, 69; Benson, *Chief Albert Lutuli*, 50; Alan Paton, *Contact*, November 2, 1961, quoted in Mary-Louise Hooper, "Profile—Albert John Luthuli," November 17, 1961, MLHP.

68. *Contact*, October 19, 1961.

69. *Natal Mercury*, October 27, 1961; Minister of Interior Jan De Klerk, press statement, November 3, 1961.

70. Peter Rule, Marilyn Aitken, and Jenny Van Dyk, *Nokukhanya: Mother of Light* (Berkeley: University of California Press, 1993), 121–23.

71. Albert Luthuli, interview, CBS Network, Oslo, December 9, 1961, in *Sabotage in South Africa*, CBS Television

documentary, U.S. broadcast in early 1962; *Rand Daily Mail,* December 12, 1961; Scott Couper, *Albert Luthuli: Bound by Faith* (Scottsville: University of Kwa-Zulu-Natal Press, 2010), 138; Eric Mtshali, interview, in Magubane et al., "The Turn to Armed Struggle," 62; *Natal Mercury,* December 8, 13, 1961.

72. Hooper notes, December 8, 1961, About and to Chief, Nok, Albertinah, etc. folder, MLHP.

73. James Allen, *Rabble-Rouser for Peace: The Authorized Biography of* Desmond Tutu (Washington, DC: Free Press, 2006), 209.

74. Scott Couper, "'An Embarrassment to the Congresses?': The Silencing of Chief Albert Luthuli and the Production of ANC History," *Journal of Southern African Studies* 35, no. 2 (2009): 340.

75. Tor Sellström, interview with Walter Sisulu, September 15, 1995, in Tor Sellström, *Sweden and National Liberation in Southern Africa,* vol. 1, *Formation of a Popular Opinion (1950–1970)* (Uppsala: Nordic Africa Institute, 1999), 178; Mandela, *Long Walk,* 360, 384.

76. Mary Benson, *A Far Cry: The Making of a South African* (Johannesburg: Ravan Press, 1996), 132–33.

77. Jeff Guy, "Imperial Appropriations: Baden-Powell, the Wood Badge and the Zulu *Iziqu,*" in Carton, Laband, and Sithole, *Zulu Identities,* 194; Raymond Suttner, "The Road to Freedom Is Via the Cross: 'Just Means' in Chief Albert Luthuli's Life," *South African Historical Journal* 62, no. 4 (2010), 693–715.

78. *Natal Mercury,* December 11, 1961.

79. Lionel Bernstein, *Memory against Forgetting: Memoirs from a Life in South African Politics, 1938–1964* (London: Viking Press, 1999), 232.

80. Callinicos, *Oliver Tambo,* 253; Lodge, *Sharpeville,* 82; Sellström, *Sweden and National Liberation,* 177–78; Denis Herbstein, *White Lies: Canon Collins and the Secret War against Apartheid* (London: James Currey, 2004), 71.

81. Smith, *Young Mandela,* 282; Sisulu Robben Island Memoir, 129; Shubin, *The ANC: A View from Moscow,* 11–12.

82. Thomas J. Karis and Gail M. Gerhart, *Challenge and Violence, 1953–1964,* vol. 3 of *From Protest to Challenge: A Docu-*

mentary History of African Politics in South Africa, 1882–1964, ed. Thomas J. Karis and Gwendolen M. Carter (Stanford: Hoover Institution Press, 1977); Magnus Gunther, "The National Committee of Liberation (NCL) African Resistance Movement (ARM)," in Magubane et al., *The Road to Democracy,* 1:241, 246–47, 249; Saul Dubow, "Were There Political Alternatives in the Wake of the Sharpeville-Langa Violence in South Africa, 1960?," *Journal of African History* 56, no. 1 (2015): 131–32.

83. Statement by the Reverend Canon L. John Collins, before the Special Political Committee of the General Assembly, October 19, 1967, E. S. Reddy Papers, Yale University Library (hereafter ESRP).

84. Couper, *Bound by Faith,* 140; Simpson, *Umkhonto,* 37–38.

85. Billy Nair, quoted in the film *Legacy of a Legend: Chief Albert J. M. Luthuli,* documentary video produced by the Department of Arts and Culture (2005).

86. Simpson, *Umkhonto,* 37–42; The State vs. Nelson Mandela, et al., 19 FO 371/177123 South Africa: Rivonia Trial, folder 2, Apartheid South Africa, 1948–66, UK NA (hereafter *State vs. Mandela*).

87. Magubane et al., "The Turn to Armed Struggle," 120. On the politics of "Dingaan's Day," see Jabulani Sithole, "Changing Meanings of the Battle of Ncome and Images of King Dingane in Twentieth-Century South Africa," in Carton, Laband, and Sithole, *Zulu Identities,* 322–30.

88. Simpson, *Umkhonto,* 46.

89. Luthuli, *Let My People,* 127.

90. Curnick Ndlovu, interview, in Magubane et al., "The Turn to Armed Struggle," 90.

91. Bunting, *Moses Kotane,* 69.

92. T. Gcabashe, interview with M. B. Yengwa, November 1973, 58, folder 112, box 6, LPSC.

93. T. Gcabashe, interview with John Reuling, 16–17, LPSC; "The Other Nobel So. Africa Winner," in "Material about Albert Luthuli," folder 35, box 5, John Reuling Papers.

94. Jordan Ngubane, *An African Explains Apartheid* (New York: Praeger Books, 1963), 108–10.

95. *New Age*, June 21, 1962.

96. Simpson, *Umkhonto*, 46; Landau, "'Turn to Violence,'" 554; Couper, *Bound by Faith*, 149–51.

97. *Golden City Post*, March 25, 1962.

98. Bonner, "The Antinomies," 44; Hugh Macmillan, *The Lusaka Years: The ANC in Exile in Zambia, 1963–1994* (Johannesburg: Jacana Press, 2013), 14–15; Sisulu Robben Island Memoir; Karis and Gerhart, *Challenge and Violence*, 648. PAFMECA convened in Addis Ababa during February 1962.

99. Mandela, *Long Walk*; Naidoo, *In the Shadow*, 72.

100. Ronnie Kasrils, *Armed and Dangerous: From Undercover Struggle to Freedom* (Auckland Park: Jacana Media, 2014), 9–50; Arianna Lissoni, "Transformations in the ANC External Mission and Umkhonto we Sizwe, c. 1960–1969," *Journal of Southern African Studies* 35, no. 2 (2009): 288, 292; Smith, *Young Mandela*, 315, 319; Naidoo, *In the Shadow*, 73–74. On CIA complicity, see *Sunday Times*, May 15, 2016; *Washington Post*, May 16, 2016.

101. Joe Matthews, interview, in Magubane et al., *Telling Their Stories*, 20.

102. Ibid., 20–21; Lissoni, "Transformations," 292.

103. George Houser, testimony to Special Committee on Apartheid, May 1963, 1963 folder, ESRP.

104. Kasrils, *Armed and Dangerous*, 40–41.

105. Colin Bundy, *Govan Mbeki* (Athens: Ohio University Press, 2012), 115; Babenia, *Memoirs of a Saboteur*, 61.

106. A. J. Eden to W. H. Young, March 10, 1964, FO 1117/2, Apartheid South Africa, 1948–66, UK NA.

107. British consul-general Anthony Eden with Albert Luthuli, Durban, August 28, 1963, Summary Despatch no. 48, September 13, 1963, FO 371/167495, UK NA.

108. Ryan Irwin, *Gordian Knot: Apartheid and the Unmaking of the Liberal World Order* (New York: Oxford University Press, 2012), 78–79; Njubi Francis Nesbitt, *Race against Sanctions: African Americans against Apartheid, 1946–1994* (Bloomington: Indiana University Press, 2004)

109. Albert Luthuli, "Appeal for Action against Apartheid," September 1962, folder 35, box 5, LPSC; "No Arms

for South Africa: An Appeal by Chief Albert J. Luthuli to the Peoples of the World," May 1963, *South Africa Freedom News*, January 1964, in folder labeled August 21, 1963–June 30, 1965, ERP.

110. Oliver Tambo, "Comments and Observations by O. R. Tambo, Deputy-President, ANC (SA) on Proposals for a Security Council (UNO) Resolution on Apartheid"; Luthuli, "No Arms for South Africa," both sources in folder labeled August 21, 1963–June 30, 1965, ERP.

111. Kathrada, *No Bread for Mandela*, 175–76; A. J. Eden, British consulate, Durban, to W. H. Young, British Embassy, Cape Town, March 10, 1964, in FO 1117/2, UK National Archives; Luthuli's letter can be found at http://www.anc.org.za/ancdocs/history/lutuli/let640309.html. ANC leader Robert Resha forwarded Luthuli's message to allies at the UN: R. Resha to E. Reddy, March 21, 1964, African National Congress 1964–79 folder, ERP.

112. Meredith, *Mandela*, 275; *Spotlight on South Africa* 2, no. 24 (1964): 2–3, "About Luthuli" folder, MLHP.

113. Kenneth Broun, *Saving Nelson Mandela: The Rivonia Trial and the Fate of South Africa* (New York: Oxford University Press, 2012), 102–15. Ahmed Kathrada was convicted on only one count, conspiracy to violate the Sabotage Act. Rusty Bernstein was acquitted on all charges. Reddy and Resha substituted language in the original document condemning the death sentence with references to life imprisonment: Vinson personal communication with E. S. Reddy, September 9, 2015; the original statement is in folder 86, box 4, LPSC.

114. "Statement by Chief Albert Luthuli on the conclusion of the Rivonia Trial, June 12, 1964," in Karis and Carter, *From Protest to Challenge*, 3:798–99.

115. Martin Luther King Jr., "Address on South African Independence," December 7, 1964, London.

116. Martin Luther King Jr., "Apartheid in South Africa," July 12, 1963, 1–3, Archives of the Martin Luther King, Jr. Center for Nonviolent Social Change, Atlanta, GA.

117. http://www.nobelprize.org/nobel_prizes/peace/laureates/1964/king-acceptance_en.html.

118. Martin Luther King Jr., "Chaos or Community: Where Do We Go from Here?," in *A Testament of Hope: The Essential Writings and Speeches of Martin Luther King, Jr.*, ed. James Washington (New York: HarperOne, 2003), 621.

119. *Johannesburg Sunday Times*, July 1962; *Baltimore Afro-American*, August 18, 1962; *Race Relations News*, December 1962; *Boston Globe*, August 1, 1962.

120. The original painting is at the South African National Gallery, and a replica is on display at the offices of the Nelson Mandela Foundation.

121. *Record* (NJ), June 16, 1964; Couper, *Bound by Faith*, 185, Gerald J. Pillay, *Voices of Liberation: Albert Luthuli* (Pretoria: HSRC Press, 1993), 22; Elinor Sisulu, *Walter and Albertina Sisulu: In Our Lifetime* (Cape Town: Abacus Books, 2003), 220; *Los Angeles Times*, June 14, 1964.

122. W. Z. Conco to Mary-Louise Hooper, March 26, 1965, Chief Lutuli and the United Nations folder, ESRP.

123. Nelson Algren, "Studs Terkel: His Secret Is Safe," *Los Angeles Times*, April 7, 1974; Rule, Aitken, and Van Dyk, *Nokukhanya*, 13, Couper, *Bound by Faith*, 184; *Washington Post*, June 9, 1966; *New York Times*, June 9, 1966.

124. Rule, Aitken, and Van Dyk, *Nokukhanya*, 137, 142.

125. Nokukhanya Luthuli to Mary-Louise Hooper, November 24, 1964, Chief Lutuli and the United Nations folder, ESRP; statement by Mary-Louise Hooper to the Special Committee on Apartheid, 13–14, 17, Chief Lutuli and the United Nations, folder, ESRP; *New York Times*, October 30, 1964; *New York Times*, October 31, 1964; *Baltimore Afro-American*, February 6, 1965. The government claimed that Luthuli had access to any doctor except any accused of being communist. "Affidavit of Dr. B. Morris, January 25, 1965, and Dr. D. A. Edington to Dr. B. Morris, January 20, 1965, About Luthuli folder, MLHP.

126. Naidoo, *In the Shadow*, 75.

127. Albert Luthuli, public statement, "The Road to Freedom Is Via the Cross," November 11, 1952, reprinted in Albert Luthuli, *Luthuli: Speeches of Chief Albert Luthuli, 1898–1967*, comp. E. S. Reddy (Durban: Madiba, 1991), 10–13.

128. H. G. M. Bass to G. E. B. Shannon, Commonwealth Relations Office, November 7, 1961, File Name, South Africa: ANC and PAC, Apartheid South Africa 1948–1966, Dominions Office (DO) 180/6..

129. Rule, Aitken, and Van Dyk, *Nokukhanya*, 140–41, 145.

130. A/Gen File No. Inq. 1778/67, Exhibits M, N, S and T, Inquest Report, Luthuli Papers, Northwestern University.

131. Nokukhanya Luthuli to Mary-Louise Hooper, August 9, 1967; Mary-Louise Hooper to Oliver Tambo, October 16, 1967, MLHP.

Coda

1. Moses Kotane, eulogy of Albert Luthuli, July 25, 1967, Mary-Louise Hooper Papers, Special Collections, Michigan State University (hereafter MLHP).

2. Statement of Rep. Barratt O'Hara, 113 Cong. Rec., July 25, 1967, 199951–52. One example of the numerous eulogies from African liberation movements is "Statement by Jacob Kuhangua, The Secretary-General of SWAPO on the Death of Chief Albert Luthuli, President of the African National Congress of S. Africa," July 24, 1967, MLHP.

3. For an authoritative account of Luthuli's funeral and *izibongo*, see Liz Gunner, "The Politics of Language and Chief Albert Luthuli's Funeral, 30 July 1967," in *One Hundred Years of the ANC: Debating Liberation Histories Today,* ed. Arianna Lissoni, Jon Soske, Natasha Erlank, Noor Nieftagodien, and Omar Badsha (Johannesburg: University of the Witwatersrand Press, 2012), 191–209. Luthuli's izibongo is reprinted in Liz Gunner and Mafika Gwala, *Musho!: Zulu Popular Praises* (East Lansing: Michigan State University Press, 1991), 80–87.

4. *Sunday Times*, August 6, 1967; Jabulani Sithole and Sibongiseni Mkhize, "Truth or Lies? Selective Memories, Imaginings and Representations of Chief Albert Luthuli in recent political discourses," *History and Theory* 39, no. 4 (1998): 69–85.

5. Forged letter, Albert Luthuli to U Thant, May 2, 1963, "Chief Lutuli and the United Nations" folder, ESRP; Luthuli

to Tambo, June 21, 1963, Chief Lutuli and the United Nations folder, ESRP .

6. Luthuli to Tambo, June 21, 1963, Chief Lutuli and the United Nations folder, ESRP.

7. Moses Kotane, eulogy of Albert Luthuli, July 25, 1967, MLHP.

8. *Rand Daily Mail*, August 1, 1967.

9. *Sechaba*, October 1967, 7. Claus von Stauffenberg was a German army officer who was a leader in a failed 1944 attempt to assassinate Adolf Hitler and remove the Nazi Party from power.

10. Stephen Ellis, *External Mission: The ANC in Exile* (Johannesburg: Jonathan Ball, 2012), 17, 27; Ellis, "Nelson Mandela, the South African Communist Party and the Origins of Umkhonto we Sizwe," *Cold War History* 16, no. 1 (2016): 17.

11. Thula Simpson, "Nelson Mandela and the Genesis of the ANC's Armed Struggle: Notes on Method," *Journal of Southern African Studies* 44, no. 1 (2018): 133–48.

12. See Thomas Borstelmann, *Apartheid's Reluctant Uncle: The United States and Southern Africa in the Early Cold War* (New York: Oxford University Press, 1993); Rob Skinner, *The Foundations of Anti-Apartheid: Liberal Humanitarianism and Transnational Activists in Britain and the U.S., c. 1919–64* (New York: Palgrave Macmillan, 2010); Ryan Irwin, *Gordian Knot: Apartheid and the Unmaking of the Liberal World Order* (New York: Oxford University Press, 2012).

13. Oliver Tambo to E. S. Reddy, August 31, 1967, Oliver Tambo correspondence folder, E. S. Reddy Papers, Yale University Library.

14. Thula Simpson, *Umkhonto we Sizwe: The ANC's Armed Struggle* (Cape Town: Penguin Press 2016), 133–66.

15. Albert Luthuli to Mary-Louise Hooper, n.d., "Memoirs S.A." folder, MLHP.

16. Julie Frederikse, *The Unbreakable Thread: Non-racialism in South Africa* (Bloomington: Indiana University Press, 1990), 266. Mandela was paraphrasing a 1958 speech by Luthuli, "Our Vision Is a Democratic Society," reprinted in Gerald

J. Pillay, *Voices of Liberation: Albert Luthuli* (Pretoria: HSRC Press, 1993), 116.

17. Peter Rule, Marilyn Aitken, and Jenny Van Dyk, *Nokukhanya: Mother of Light* (Berkeley: University of California Press, 1993), 173.

Bibliography

Books

Allen, James. *Rabble-Rouser for Peace: The Authorized Biography of* Desmond Tutu. Washington, DC: Free Press, 2006.

Anthony, David. *Max Yergan: Race Man, Internationalist, Cold Warrior.* New York: New York University Press, 2006.

Asmal, Kader. *Politics in My Blood: A Memoir.* Johannesburg: Jacana Press, 2011.

Asmal, Kader, David Chidester, and Wilmot James, eds. *South Africa's Nobel Laureates: Peace, Literature and Science.* Johannesburg: Jonathan Ball, 2004.

Babenia, Natoo. *Memoirs of a Saboteur: Reflections on My Political Activity in India and South Africa.* Cape Town: Mayibuye Books, 1995.

Benson, Mary. *The African Patriots: The Story of the African National Congress of South Africa.* London: Faber and Faber, 1963.

———. *Chief Albert Lutuli of South Africa.* London: Oxford University Press, 1963.

———. *A Far Cry: The Making of a South African.* London: Penguin Books, 1996.

Bernstein, Lionel. *Memory against Forgetting: Memoirs from a Life in South African Politics, 1938–1964.* London: Viking Press, 1999.

Borstelmann, Thomas. *Apartheid's Reluctant Uncle: The United States and Southern Africa in the Early Cold War.* New York: Oxford University Press, 1993.

Broun, Kenneth. *Saving Nelson Mandela: The Rivonia Trial and the Fate of South Africa.* New York: Oxford University Press, 2012.

Bundy, Colin. *Govan Mbeki.* Athens: Ohio University Press, 2012.

Bunting, Brian. *Moses Kotane, South African Revolutionary: A Political Biography.* London: Inkululeko Press, 1975.

Callan, Edward. *Albert John Luthuli and the South African Race Conflict.* Kalamazoo: Western Michigan University Press, 1962.

Callinicos, Luli. *Oliver Tambo: Beyond the Engeli Mountains.* Cape Town: David Philip, 2004.

Carton, Benedict, John Laband, and Jabulani Sithole, eds. *Zulu Identities: Being Zulu, Past and Present.* Pietermaritzburg: University of Kwa-Zulu-Natal, 2008.

Chidester, David. *Religions of South Africa.* London: Routledge, 1992 [2014].

Cope, Nicholas. *To Bind the Nation: Solomon kaDinuzulu and Zulu Nationalism, 1913–1933.* Scottsville: University of Kwa-Zulu-Natal Press, 1997.

Couper, Scott. *Albert Luthuli: Bound by Faith.* Scottsville: University of Kwa-Zulu-Natal Press, 2010.

De Klerk, F. W. *The Last Trek—A New Beginning.* New York: St. Martin's Press, 1998.

Delius, Peter. *Sebatakgomo, Migrant Organization, the ANC and the Sekhukuneland Revolt.* Johannesburg: University of Witwatersrand Press, 1990.

Drew, Allison, ed. *South Africa's Radical Tradition: A Documentary History.* Vol. 2, *1943–1964.* Cape Town: Buchu Books, 1997.

Dubow, Saul. *Apartheid, 1948–1994.* Oxford: Oxford University Press, 2014.

———. *The African National Congress.* Johannesburg: Jonathan Ball, 2000.

Edgar, Robert R., and Luyanda ka Msumza, eds. *Africa's Cause Must Triumph: The Collected Writings of A.P. Mda.* Johannesburg: HSRC Press, 2018.

Ellis, Stephen. *External Mission: The ANC in Exile, 1960–1990.* Oxford: Oxford University Press, 2013.

Elphick, Richard. *The Equality of Believers: Protestant Missionaries and the Racial Politics of South Africa.* Charlottesville: University of Virginia Press, 2012.

Elphick, Richard, and Rodney Davenport, eds. *Christianity in South Africa: A Political, Social and Cultural History.* Cape Town: David Philip, 1997.

Etherington, Norman. *Preachers, Peasants and Politics in Southern Africa, 1835–1880: African Christian Communities in Natal, Pondoland and Zululand.* London: Royal Historical Society, 1978.

Everatt, David. *The Origins of Non-racialism.* Johannesburg: University of Witwatersrand Press, 2010.

Fanon, Frantz. *Wretched of the Earth.* New York: Grove Press, 1963.

Feinberg, Harvey. *Our Land, Our Life, Our Future: Black South African Challenges to Territorial Segregation, 1913–1948.* Pretoria: UNISA Press, 2015.

Field, Connie. *Have You Heard from Johannesburg: Seven Stories from the Global Anti-apartheid Movement.* Berkeley, CA: Clarity Films, 2010.

Frankel, Philip. *An Ordinary Atrocity: Sharpeville and Its Massacre.* New Haven: Yale University Press, 2001.

Frederikse, Julie. The Unbreakable Thread: Non-racialism in South Africa. Bloomington: Indiana University Press, 1990.

From Protest to Challenge: A Documentary History of African Politics in South Africa, 1882–1964. 6 vols. Edited by Thomas J. Karis and Gwendolen M. Carter (vols. 1–4). Stanford: Hoover Institution Press (vols. 1–4); Bloomington: Indiana University Press (vols. 5–6), 1972–2010.

Gerhart, Gail M. *Black Power: The Evolution of an Ideology.* Berkeley: University of California Press, 1978.

Gerhart, Gail M., and Thomas J. Karis. *Political Profiles.* Vol. 4 of *From Protest to Challenge.*

Giliomee, Hermann. *The Afrikaners: A Biography of a People.* Charlottesville: University of Virginia Press, 2009.

———. *The Last Afrikaner Leaders: A Supreme Test of Power.* Charlottesville: University of Virginia Press, 2012.

Gish, Steven. *Alfred B. Xuma: African, American, South African.* New York: NYU Press, 2000.

Gordimer, Nadine. *Telling Times: Writing and Living, 1954–2008.* New York: W. W. Norton, 2010.

Graybill, Lynn. *Religion and Resistance Politics in South Africa.* Westport, CT: Praeger Press, 1995.

Gunner, Elizabeth, and Mafika Gwala. *Musho!: Zulu Popular Praises.* East Lansing: Michigan State University Press, 1991.

Harrison, Ronald. *The Black Christ: A Journey to Freedom.* Cape Town: David Philip, 2006.

Hepple, Bob. *Young Man with a Red Tie: A Memoir of Mandela and the Failed Revolution, 1960–1963.* Auckland Park: Jacana Media, 2013.

Herbstein, Denis. *White Lies: Canon Collins and the Secret War against Apartheid.* London: James Currey, 2004.

Houle, Robert. *Making African Christianity: Africans Reimagining Their Faith in Colonial Southern Africa.* Bethlehem, PA: Lehigh University Press, 2011.

Houser, George. *No One Can Stop the Rain.* Cleveland: Pilgrim Press, 1989.

Houser, George, and Herbert Shore. *I Will Go Singing: Walter Sisulu Speaks of His Life and Struggle for Freedom in South Africa in Conversation with George Houser and Herbert Shore.* Cape Town: Robben Island Museum, 2001.

Huddleston, Trevor. *Naught for Your Comfort.* Johannesburg: Hardingham and Donaldson, 1956.

Irwin, Ryan. *Gordian Knot: Apartheid and the Unmaking of the Liberal World Order.* New York: Oxford University Press, 2012.

Johns, Sheridan, and R. Hunt Davis, eds. *Mandela, Tambo and the African National Congress: The Struggle against Apartheid, 1948–1990; A Documentary Survey.* Oxford: Oxford University Press, 1991.

Joseph, Helen. *If This Be Treason.* New York: Contra Mundum Press, 1998.

Karis, Thomas J. *Hope and Challenge, 1935–1952.* Vol. 2 of *From Protest to Challenge.*

Karis, Thomas J., and Gail M. Gerhart. *Challenge and Violence, 1953–1964.* Vol. 3 of *From Protest to Challenge.*

———. *Nadir and Resurgence, 1964–1979*. Vol. 5 of *From Protest to Challenge*.

Kasrils, Ronnie. *Armed and Dangerous: From Undercover Struggle to Freedom*. Auckland Park: Jacana Media, 2014.

Kathrada, Ahmed. *No Bread for Mandela: Memoirs of Ahmed Kathrada, Prisoner No. 468/64*. Lexington: University of Kentucky Press, 2011.

Kenney, Henry. *Architect of Apartheid: H. F. Verwoerd—An Appraisal*. Johannesburg: Jonathan Ball, 1980.

La Hausse de Lalouviere, Paul. *Restless Identities: Signatures of Nationalism, Zulu Ethnicity and History in the Lives of Petros Lamula (c. 1881–1948) and Lymon Maling (1889–c. 1936)*. Pietermaritzburg: University of Kwa-Zulu-Natal Press, 2000.

Legum, Colin, and Margaret Legum. *The Bitter Choice: Eight South Africans' Resistance to Tyranny*. New York: World, 1968.

Lembede, Anton Muziwakhe. *Freedom in Our Lifetime: The Collected Writings of Anton Muziwakhe Lembede*. Edited by Robert R. Edgar and Luyanda ka Msumza. Athens: Ohio University Press, 1996.

Limb, Peter. *The ANC's Early Years: Nation, Class and Place in South Africa before 1940*. Pretoria: UNISA Press, 2010.

Lodge, Tom. *Black Politics in South Africa since 1945*. Johannesburg: Ravan Press, 1983.

———. *Mandela: A Critical Life*. New York: Oxford University Press, 2006.

———. *Sharpeville: An Apartheid Massacre and Its Consequences*. Oxford: Oxford University Press, 2011.

Luthuli, Albert. *Let My People Go*. New York: McGraw-Hill, 1962.

———. *Luthuli: Speeches of Chief Albert Luthuli, 1898–1967*. Comp. E. S. Reddy. Durban: Madiba, 1991.

Macmillan, Hugh. *The Lusaka Years: The ANC in Exile in Zambia, 1963–1994*. Johannesburg: Jacana Press, 2013.

Magubane, Bernard, et al. *The Road to Democracy in South Africa*. 6 vols. Pretoria: UNISA Press, 2005–13.

———. *The Road to Democracy in South Africa: South Africans Telling Their Stories.* Vol. 1, *1950–1970.* Pretoria: UNISA Press, 2008.

Mandela, Nelson. *Conversations with Myself.* New York: Picador Press, 2011.

———. *Long Walk to Freedom.* Boston: Little Brown, 1994.

Marks, Shula. *The Ambiguities of Dependence in South Africa: Class, Nationalism and the State in Twentieth-Century Natal.* Johannesburg: Ravan Press, 1986.

———. *Reluctant Rebellion: The 1906–8 Disturbances in Natal.* Oxford: Clarendon Press, 1970.

Mbeki, Govan. *South Africa: The Peasant's Revolt.* London: Penguin, 1964.

Meer, Ismail. A Fortunate Man. Cape Town: Struik, 2002.

Meredith, Martin. *Mandela: A Biography.* New York: Public Affairs Books, 2011.

Mesthrie, Uma. *Gandhi's Prisoner? The Life of Gandhi's Son Manilal.* Cape Town: Kwela Books, 2004.

Naidoo, Logan. *In the Shadow of Chief Luthuli: Reflections of Goolam Suleiman.* Groutville: Luthuli Museum, 2010.

Nesbitt, Njubi Francis. *Race against Sanctions: African Americans against Apartheid, 1946–1994.* Bloomington: Indiana University Press, 2004.

Ngubane, Jordan. *An African Explains Apartheid.* New York: Praeger Books, 1963.

Odendaal, Andre. *The Founders: The Origins of the ANC and the Struggle for Democracy in South Africa.* Lexington: University of Kentucky Press, 2013.

Pillay, Gerald J. *Voices of Liberation: Albert Luthuli.* Pretoria: HSRC Press, 1993.

Pogrund, Benjamin. *Robert Sobukwe: How Can Man Die Better.* Johannesburg: Jonathan Ball Press, 2015.

Rule, Peter, Marilyn Aitken, and Jenny Van Dyk. *Nokukhanya: Mother of Light.* Berkeley: University of California Press, 1993.

Sampson, Anthony. *Mandela.* London: HarperCollins, 2011.

———. *The Treason Cage: The Opposition on Trial in South Africa.* London: Heinemann, 1958.

Sellström, Tor. *Sweden and National Liberation in Southern Africa*. Vol. 1, *Formation of a Popular Opinion (1950–1970)*. Uppsala: Nordic Africa Institute, 1999.

Shubin, Vladimir. The ANC: A View from Moscow. Johannesburg: Jacana Press, 2009.

Skinner, Rob. *The Foundations of Anti-Apartheid: Liberal Humanitarianism and Transnational Activists in Britain and the U.S., c. 1919–64*. New York: Palgrave Macmillan, 2010.

Simpson, Thula, ed. *The ANC and the Liberation Struggle in South Africa: Essential Writings*. London: Routledge Press, 2017.

———. *Umkhonto we Sizwe: The ANC's Armed Struggle*. Cape Town: Penguin Random House, 2016.

Sisulu, Elinor. *Walter and Albertina Sisulu: In Our Lifetime*. Cape Town: Abacus Books, 2003.

Slovo, Joe. *The Unfinished Autobiography of ANC Leader Joe Slovo*. Melbourne: Ocean Press, 2002.

Smith, David James. *Young Mandela*. Boston: Little, Brown, 2010.

Soske, Jon. *Internal Frontiers: African Nationalism and the Indian Diaspora in Twentieth-Century South Africa*. Athens: Ohio University Press, 2017.

———. "'Wash Me Black Again': African Nationalism, the Indian Diaspora, and Kwa-Zulu Natal, 1944–1960." PhD diss., University of Toronto, 2009.

Stengel, Richard. *Mandela's Way: Lessons on Life, Love, and Courage*. Danvers, MA: Crown Archetype Books, 2010.

Suttner, Raymond. *The ANC Underground in South Africa*. Johannesburg: Jacana Media, 2008.

———. *Recovering Democracy in South Africa*. Boulder, CO: Lynne Rienner, 2015.

Suttner, Raymond, and Jeremy Cronin, eds. *50 Years of the Freedom Charter*. Pretoria: UNISA Press, 2006.

Temkin, Ben. *Buthelezi: A Biography*. London: Routledge, 2013.

Turok, Ben. *Nothing but the Truth: Behind the ANC's Struggle Politics*. Johannesburg: Jonathan Ball, 2003.

Veerwoerd, Hendrik. *Verwoerd Speaks: Speeches, 1948–1966.* Edited by A. N. Pelzer. Johannesburg: APB, 1966.

Villa-Vicencio, Charles, ed. *Theology and Violence: The South African Debate.* Grand Rapids: Eerdmans, 1988.

Welsh, David. *The Rise and Fall of Apartheid.* Charlottesville: University of Virginia Press, 2009.

Essays and Journal Articles

Alegi, Peter. "Sport, Race, and Liberation: A Preliminary Study of Albert Luthuli's Sporting Life." In *Sport and Liberation in South Africa: Reflections and Suggestions,* edited by Cornelius Thomas, 66–82. Alice: University of Fort Hare Press, 2006.

Bank, Leslie, and Benedict Carton. "Forgetting Apartheid: History, Culture and the Body of a Nun." *Africa* 86, no. 3 (2016): 472–503.

Benneyworth, Garth. "Armed and Trained: Nelson Mandela's 1962 Military Mission as Commander in Chief of Umkhonto we Sizwe and Provenance for His Buried Makarov Pistol." *South African Historical Journal* 63, no. 1 (2011): 78–101.

Bonner, Philip. "The Antinomies of Nelson Mandela." In *The Cambridge Companion to Nelson Mandela,* edited by Rita Barnard, 29–49. New York: Cambridge University Press, 2014.

Carton, Benedict. "Awaken Nkunkulu, Zulu God of the Old Testament: Pioneering Missionaries during the Early Age of Racial Spectacle." In Carton, Laband, and Sithole, *Zulu Identities,* 133–52.

Carton, Benedict, and Rob Morrell. "Competitive Combat, Warrior Bodies, and Zulu Sport: The Gender Relations of Stick Fighting in South Africa, 1800–1930." In *Beyond C. L. R. James: Shifting Boundaries of Race and Ethnicity in Sport,* edited by John Nauright, Alan Cobley, and David Wiggins, 125–44. Fayetteville: University of Arkansas Press, 2014.

Couper, Scott Everett. "Emasculating Agency: An Unambiguous Assessment of Albert Luthuli's Stance on Violence." *South African Historical Journal* 64, no. 3 (2012): 564–86.

———. "'An Embarrassment to the Congresses?': The Silencing of Chief Albert Luthuli and the Production of ANC History." *Journal of Southern African Studies* 35, no. 2 (2009): 331–48.

———. "When Chief Albert Luthuli Launched 'Into the Deep': A Theological Reflection on a Homiletic Resource of Political Significance." *Journal of Theology for Southern Africa* 130 (March 2008): 76–89.

Dubow, Saul. "Were There Political Alternatives in the Wake of the Sharpeville-Langa Violence in South Africa, 1960?" *Journal of African History* 56, no. 1 (2015): 119–42.

Edgar, Robert, and Myra Ann Houser. "'The Most Patient of Animals, Next to the Ass': Jan Smuts, Howard University, and African American Leadership, 1930." *Safundi* 18, no. 1 (2017): 29–51.

Ellis, Stephen. "The Genesis of the ANC's Armed Struggle in South Africa, 1948–1961." *Journal of Southern African Studies* 37, no. 4 (2011): 657–76.

———. "Nelson Mandela, the South African Communist Party and the Origins of Umkhonto we Sizwe." *Cold War History* 16, no. 1 (2016): 1–17.

Gunner, Elizabeth. "The Politics of Language and Chief Albert Luthuli's Funeral, 30 July 1967." In *One Hundred Years of the ANC: Debating Liberation Histories Today,* edited by Arianna Lissoni, Jon Soske, Natasha Erlank, Noor Nieftagodien, and Omar Badsha, 191–209. Johannesburg: University of the Witwatersrand Press, 2012.

Guy, Jeff. "Imperial Appropriations: Baden-Powell, the Wood Badge and the Zulu Iziqu." In Carton, Laband, and Sithole, *Zulu Identities,* 193–213.

King, Martin Luther, Jr. "Chaos or Community: Where Do We Go from Here?" In *A Testament of Hope: The Essential Writings and Speeches of Martin Luther King, Jr.,* edited by James M. Washington, 555–633. New York: HarperOne, 2003.

Landau, Paul S. "The ANC, MK, and 'The Turn to Violence' (1960–1962)." *South African Historical Journal* 64, no. 3 (2012): 538–63.

———. "Controlled by Communists? (Re)Assessing the ANC in Its Exilic Decades." *South African Historical Journal* 67, no. 2 (2015): 222–41.

Lissoni, Arianna. "Transformations in the ANC External Mission and Umkhonto we Sizwe, c. 1960–1969." *Journal of Southern African Studies* 35, no. 2 (2009): 287–301.

Lodge, Tom. "Secret Party: South African Communists between 1950 and 1960." *South African Historical Journal* 67, no. 4 (2015): 433–64.

Luthuli, Albert. "Let Us Speak Together of Freedom." *Native Teachers' Journal, Fighting Talk* 10, no. 10 (1954): 4–5.

———. "Natal Native Teachers' Union." *Natal Teachers' Journal* 12, no. 1 (1932): 50–51.

———. "The Vernacular as a Medium of Instruction." *Native Teachers' Journal* 14, no. 2 (1934): 30–34.

Simpson, Thula. "Nelson Mandela and the Genesis of the ANC's Armed Struggle: Notes on Method." *Journal of Southern African Studies* 44, no. 1 (2018): 133–48.

Sithole, Jabulani. "Changing Meanings of the Battle of Ncome and Images of King Dingane in Twentieth-Century South Africa." In Carton, Laband, and Sithole, *Zulu Identities*, 322–30.

———. "Chief Albert Luthuli and Bantustan Politics." In Carton, Laband, and Sithole, *Zulu Identities*, 331–40.

Sithole, Jabulani, and Sibongiseni Mkhize. "Truth or Lies? Selective Memories, Imaginings and Representations of Chief Albert Luthuli in Recent Political Discourses." *History and Theory* 39, no. 4 (2000): 69–85.

Soske, Jon. "How to Approach Heaven." *Chimurenga Chronic,* April 5, 2016. http://chimurengachronic.co.za/how-to-approach-heaven-2/.

———. "The Impossible Concept: Settler Liberalism, Pan-Africanism, and the Language of Non-Racialism." *African Historical Review* 47, no. 2 (2015): 1–36.

———. Suttner, Raymond. "'The Road to Freedom Is Via the Cross': 'Just Means' in Chief Albert Luthuli's Life." *South African Historical Journal* 62, no. 4 (2010): 693–715.

Vinson, Robert Trent, and Benedict Carton. "Albert Luthuli's
Private Struggle: How an Icon of Peace Came to Accept
Sabotage in South Africa." *Journal of African History* 58,
no. 1 (2018): 1–28.

South African and US Newspapers and Periodicals

Advance
Baltimore Afro-American
Bantu World
Boston Globe
Christian Science Monitor
Cleveland Call and Post
Commonwealth News
Contact
Counter Attack
Daily Dispatch (Eastern Cape)
Drum
Fighting Talk
Golden City Post
Ilanga lase Natal
Indian Opinion
Inkundla ya Bantu
Iso Lomuzi
Johannesburg Sunday Times
Liberation: A Journal of Democratic Discussion
Los Angeles Times
Natal Daily News
Natal Mercury
New Age
New Journal and Guide
New York Times
Our Age
Philadelphia Tribune
Race Relations
Rand Daily Mail
Record (NJ)
Sechaba

South Africa Freedom News
Spark
Spotlight on South Africa
Star (Johannesburg)
Sunday Express
Sunday Times
Sunday Tribune
Washington Post
Wall Street Journal
World

Archival Sources

African National Congress online archives, http://www.anc
.co.org.za

African National Congress Headquarters, Archives Division,
Johannesburg, South Africa

Alan Paton Centre and Struggle Archives, University of Kwa-
Zulu Natal, Pietermaritzburg, South Africa

Aluka: Africa Action Archive, http://www.aluka.org

American Congregational Association Archives, Boston, MA

American Board of Commissioners for Foreign Missions,
Houghton Library, Harvard University, Cambridge, MA

Amistad Research Center, American Committee on Africa
Collection, Tulane University, New Orleans, LA

Bailey's African Photo Archives, Johannesburg, South Africa

Digital National Security Archive, http://searchproquest
.commutexgmu.edu/disa/docview

Killie Campbell Africana Library, Campbell Collections, University of KwaZulu-Natal, Durban, South Africa

Luthuli Museum Archives, Groutville, South Africa

Martin Luther King Jr. Center for Nonviolent Social Change,
Archival Division, Atlanta, GA

Michigan State University
  Mary-Louise Hooper Papers
  George Houser Papers
  John and Eleanor Reuling Papers

National Archives, UK

Dominions Office (DO) 119/1180 Intelligence Organisations in High Commission Territories, 1953–55

DO 180/6 South Africa: ANC and PAC, Apartheid South Africa 1948–66.

Nobel Committee, Nobel Peace Prize, http://www.nobelprizes.com

Northwestern University, Cooperative Africana Microfilm Project (CAMP)

Albert Luthuli Papers

Robben Island Mayibuye Archives, University of the Western Cape, Cape Town, South Africa

Schomburg Center for Research in Black Culture, New York Public Library, New York, NY

Albert Luthuli Papers

Phelps Stokes Papers

South African National Archives Repository, Pretoria

University of South Africa Library, Archives, Documentation Centre for African Studies, Pretoria, South Africa

William Cullen Library, Historical Papers Research Archive, University of the Witwatersrand, Johannesburg, South Africa

Yale University, New Haven, CT

Divinity Library Special Papers, John and Eleanor Reuling Papers

Enuga S. Reddy Papers

Index

CPSIA information can be obtained
at www.ICGtesting.com
Printed in the USA
FSHW020315070320
67788FS